SPARK CLICK GO

HOW TO BRING YOUR CREATIVE BUSINESS IDEA TO LIFE

© 2021 Douglas Ross

All rights reserved. Printed in the United States of America. The trademark for SPARK-CLICK-GO™ has been applied for.

Disclaimer: The stories and information in this book are true and accurate to the best of the author's and publisher's knowledge. All recommendations are made without guarantee and should not be considered as advice for any particular business or reader's situation. The author and publisher disclaim any liability in connection with the use of this information.

Cover and illustrations by Matt Davis, Very Much So Agency
Interior design by Megan McCullough
Editing by Sandra Wendel, Write On, Inc.
Author photograph by John Hall Portraits

ISBN (paperback): 978-1-7364735-0-4
ISBN (ebook): 978-1-7364735-1-1
ISBN (audiobook): 978-1-7364735-2-8

Published by D. Ross & Associates, LLC
Visit at www.sparkclickgo.com.

To Dad

Contents

Introduction 1

1 Why SPARK-CLICK-GO? 5

2 Imagination Gone Wild 11

3 One Foot in Front of the Other 19

4 The Shape of Things to Come 27

5 Let's Talk 39

6 What's Your Problem? 53

7 A Work in Progress 69

8 Blood, Sweat, and Fears 79

9 Promises, Promises 93

10 Perpetual Money-Making Machine 107

11 Build It and They Will Come 125

12 Ten, Nine, Eight 135

13 Go Forth and Multiply 145

14 Gettin' Better All the Time 161

15 Fuel Your Venture 171

16 Stop Thinking about [BIG] Venture Capital 183

17 Got Talent? 191

18 Bloopers and Blunders 201

19 Three Points at the Buzzer 209

20 Beyond SPARK-CLICK-GO 215

Bonus: How to Find a Creative Business Idea 219

SPARK-CLICK-GO FAQs 239

Acknowledgments 243

About the Author 247

Introduction

When I was a kid, growing up near the foothills of the Canadian Rockies, Reese's Peanut Butter Cups were all the rage. My neighbor and I, let's call him Phil (since that was his name), thought hmmm, maybe we could make our own peanut butter and chocolate confections and sell them to our schoolmates.

SPARK.

"Let's make a batch and see how they taste," suggested Phil. I said, "Sure."

So we asked our moms for advice (and ingredients) and got to work. We tried various types of chocolate chips in different amounts with Phil's favorite peanut butter, then with my favorite.

We had a blast making these batches because it was part of a money-making adventure we were both keen on.

The first attempts did not work out so well. The chocolate was too bitter, we didn't melt it enough, and we didn't know how to get the ingredients to mold nicely to the baking cups without sticking. Before long we figured out that spraying the paper cups with nonstick aerosol and then freezing the trays worked well.

With a bit of trial and error we created something we thought was really tasty, and so did the many brother and sister tasters that populated our respective houses.

CLICK.

The technique we came up with was simple: melt the chocolate with butter, pour into cupcake molds lined with presprayed baking cups, add a dab of peanut butter, cover with more molten chocolate, and place in the freezer overnight. Yum, I can smell the melting chocolate now.

Not only did we create a clear and simple production method, our cost of goods was zero. Nada. We implored our moms to pick up ever larger quantities of ingredients and supplies, and they indulged us. Our overhead was also zero—we did not receive a bill for electricity or for the use of the kitchen, stove, freezer, or ingredients.

When we felt ready for prime time, we took a small batch of what we had dubbed Rossnd's Peanut Butter Cups—which was an amalgam of our last names—to school and sold them at recess.

GO.

Our venture was a smash hit, and we had an infinite return on our financial investment since any amount of revenue, divided by zero costs = infinity.

Phil and I had done it. We had successfully taken a creative business idea from initial thought, through the prototyping, branding, business modeling stages, right through to launch.

We didn't know we were following a phased approach to business success then, and we didn't care, but we had. We were ambitious, ready to experiment, and we put ourselves out there to our friends and family. We were kids on a mission.

I've come up with a lot of creative business ideas over the years, run businesses, been part of early start-up teams, mentored early-stage companies, and consulted to teams in Fortune 500 companies on brand strategy, innovation, and execution.

I've heard about many seemingly creative business ideas from friends and associates. Many of these ideas are never formed into an offering that gets tested, unlike my peanut butter cup venture. Most do not become actual businesses. And that's a shame.

I'd like to see more creative business ideas, your ideas, become reality. That's why I wrote this book.

SPARK-CLICK-GO is a journey that countless entrepreneurs and creative people of all stripes have taken en route to success. By sharing this journey with you, and the stories of people who have taken this journey, my aim is to inspire you to do the same as you bring your creative business idea to life.

A creative business idea is one through which you deploy imaginative or original ideas to bring value to others and to society and that uniquely reflects and benefits its creators. Helping you find and develop a creative business idea that's right for you is the purpose of this book.

The better able you are to shape, prove, and build support and anticipation for your offering, the better able you will be to attract funding and talent when you need it. But it takes some forethought, planning, and action to garner the resources and attract the people you need, when you need them. So I've made sure to include sections on funding and talent.

The book is laid out with the logic of SPARK-CLICK-GO—each phase having multiple steps for you to navigate. It looks like a pathway of stepping-stones over the surface of a river ready to help you get to the other side, and it is, but the method is also not so rigid.

As when crossing a river, you may need to step back to that bigger, flatter, more stable rock, and rechart your course across. And like any ambitious kid, you'll skip a rock or two on occasion, and that's okay.

Whether you read every chapter, or you hop from one to the next, you'll get the most from this book if you reflect and act on what you are reading about at the end of each chapter.

Following this phased approach to creativity—common to innovation across fields including music and the arts—will help you identify, shape, test, and launch a successful creative business idea all your own.

1
Why SPARK-CLICK-GO?

Why SPARK-CLICK-GO? The short answer: without SPARK-CLICK-GO, aspiring entrepreneurs like you may remain just that—aspiring. You may waste time or money. You may struggle. You may get discouraged and re-up to a corporate life that zaps you of your creative energy.

But what if you could learn the steps along a path to creating a lasting business—one that could meet your financial needs—one that could even become something really big?

The SPARK-CLICK-GO Journey is designed to help you develop a worthy creative business—one that reflects you as a person and brings value to customers and to society.

What do you need to bring to the table? A desire to learn, to build, and an adventurer's mindset. It's going to be a ton of work—like anything worthwhile in life—so you'll want to know you are taking the right steps.

That's where SPARK-CLICK-GO comes in.

Has this ever happened to you? You come up with a brilliant idea for a business, and then ... nothing happens. Your idea goes nowhere. It lives in your thoughts or you have some fun talking about it with your friends or your partner, but your idea dies along the way. Cause of death? Lack of action.

Before getting too far along, I'd like to tackle some myths about creativity and entrepreneurship.

You may be thinking, or have heard, that entrepreneurship requires a special person—it does. You. Maybe you've heard that building a business is challenging and requires a lot of personal energy—it does. Or perhaps you have the view that it is only for the bold, the talented, or the lucky. So be bold, with the talent you have, and fill in where you have gaps. Make your own luck.

Common to all of these thoughts is a mindset that is holding you back from jumping into the fray. The truth is, any of these reasons could stop you from becoming an entrepreneur if you let them.

Many culprits get in the way. You've heard them time and again. Fear. Doubt. Procrastination. Lack. These four kill countless ideas in their infancy every day. They rob all of us—myself included—of the joy of creation. And that is why there are tons of remedies out there to help you quell these menaces.

Two books I recommend on the subject of avoiding creative distractions and focusing your mental energy are Steven Pressfield's *The War of Art: Break Through the Blocks and Win Your Inner Creative Battles* and David Kadavy's *The Heart to Start: Stop Procrastinating and Start Creating*.

Whether ideas come easily to you, or you need help coming up with a worthy idea, you still need to figure out how to bring that idea into reality. That's why I've written this book. We need more people like you developing their ideas.

My purpose is to inspire, to inform, and to show you a simple, powerful method for developing your ideas, determining if your ideas are worth pursuing, and showing you a path forward that works in most fields of endeavor—one that will raise your odds of success—so that you can bring those ideas to life.

SPARK-CLICK-GO is an easy-to-remember phrase crafted to capture the key steps an aspiring entrepreneur follows to bring an idea from concept to reality. Think about that for a moment. I'm suggesting these three components represent a pattern aspiring entrepreneurs around the world follow in bringing their endeavors to society. It's a big claim. One I intend to live up to—so keep me honest.

The words I have chosen to capture this journey are words you hear every day describing the essential components of innovation. Perhaps you've heard phrases like these:

> "The idea hit me like a flash or a SPARK."

> "I started creating beers with a twist of citrus and they CLICKed with customers right away."

> "I thought, hmmm, maybe I could start giving clown lessons online and charging people to participate, so I did, and everything CLICKed into place."

> "This is the one. Let's GO with it."

I'm guessing you will hear these words more now that you are seeing and reading them here, arranged as SPARK-CLICK-GO™.

To bring a creative business idea to life is to break the bonds of inertia, which is the tendency to stay where you are now in your life or in your career. Breaking the bonds of inertia is like making something out of nothing. It takes energy and a bias for action.

The words *SPARK*, *CLICK*, and *GO* have positive, active meanings.

SPARK may bring an image of fire to mind. The ability to make and control fire started humans on a journey toward civilization. CLICK may get you thinking about the click of fingers snapping in unison. And GO may have you picturing a train leaving a station.

Taking an idea from initial SPARK through to building something, sharing it with people, and running with it is both a journey and a skill set you can learn. It requires what I call an adventurer's mindset.

Let me explain the many benefits of embarking on the SPARK-CLICK-GO Journey.

For starters, you will create a useful product. When you go through the process of building something, you learn how to build it better. You will earn a financial return, or you will make connections that could lead you to solid financial returns.

It doesn't matter early on if you make a lot of money or a small sum. For Thomas Edison the sale was "proof of utility, and utility (was) success." If you do not make money, you will at least be seen as a player in the field.

My hope is that even one of these benefits will be enough to get you up and out of your chair and thrust you onto the playing field. Creating something of value, anything, takes skill, planning, hard work, and luck.

Making something tangible means it has a chance of outliving you. Why not, then, leave the products of your work—and who you are as a person—so that others may remember you by them? It seems morbid but think about it: we know actors by their films, master painters by their masterpieces, inventors by their products.

When you release your creative work to the world, others can build on it. And thank God for that. How would we be living now if the internet had remained solely for the benefit of the military?

If your work is in the public domain, and you have protected it from being copied, others may reference it or be inspired by it and society may benefit. In contrast, if your idea remains solely in your mind or on paper in a drawer or locked in a cloud folder only you can access, there is zero chance that society will gain. For society to gain, it means people are benefiting from the use or enjoyment of your offering—even if it's just peanut butter cups—and this is the main reason to complete the journey.

Had Leonardo da Vinci not painted the *Mona Lisa*, instead only completing studies of her, would the world be benefiting now? The same can be said about bringing your creative business idea to the world.

Bringing your creative business idea to life will be a rewarding journey. It's going to take a lot of diligence and agility. You will experience ups and downs. That's why it is essential that you bring something of yourself to the table, to focus on something you want to see in the world, and to solve a problem you are passionate about.

You're going to need the intestinal fortitude.

2
Imagination Gone Wild

You may be wondering what sets a creative business idea apart from a regular business idea, and why it matters. Let's take a look.

A creative business idea is about purpose and profit. It uniquely reflects the person who creates it *and* returns a profit. If you were to take a moment to look up the definition of *business*, you would find answers like these:

- The practice of making one's living by engaging in commerce
- The state of being busy
- The organized efforts and activities of individuals to sell goods and services for profit

These definitions reflect what humans collectively have been doing since before the invention of money—and especially since the Industrial Revolution—yet something is missing from this transactional depiction—*you*.

Not *you* specifically, I'm speaking of the primacy of the individual—a person's background, skills, talents, desires, interests. I'm speaking of the qualities that make a person unique. Connecting this essence of what makes you unique to the creation of a product, service, or a creative production that brings value to others is what I'm talking about.

A creative business idea (CBI) deploys imaginative, or original ideas, to deliver value for others and for society, profitably, while uniquely reflecting and benefiting its creators.

A CBI is not the same as what some people would call a *lifestyle business*—meaning, a business that allows its owner to make just enough money to sustain a desired lifestyle, with minimal effort. Some lifestyle businesses are creative businesses, but not all. And some creative business ideas become big businesses over time.

A creative business idea deploys imaginative or original ideas and reflects the uniqueness of its creators. Think about that for a moment. What would it mean to deploy imaginative or original ideas in bringing about a business?

To be imaginative is to picture something you would like to see in the world as a business, something that stands out from other businesses that exist now in a category, and then figuring out how to make it real.

To use original ideas in the creation of a business is a high hurdle to achieve, but in doing so your idea will stand out from the crowd. Push yourself to create a business based on a verifiably, and possibly patentable, original idea, or bring something original to your idea, even if it is a twist on an old theme.

Most people would agree that a business capable of 3-D printing human organs is deploying original ideas. But so, too, would be the creation of the first coffee franchise built on human-first, 100 percent sustainable coffee, supplies and other ingredients, renewable energy for its operations, and zero non-usable waste.

Deploying original or imaginative ideas is not meant to be a bar that only a person with Herculean strength or Einsteinian intellect can surmount. It is intended to get aspiring entrepreneurs like you to stretch your thinking—

and your ambition—so you can bring something fresh to the world in an existing category or to create a new category.

Look at Apple. Much of their success is based on the use of imaginative ideas such as creating easy-to-use operating systems, elegant devices, and brilliant branding, but their success is not necessarily based on original ideas. At nearly $2 trillion in market cap (circa August 2020), they are doing okay.

A franchisee does not deploy original or imaginative ideas since someone else has done all the creative work developing, testing, and refining the concept. If you want to become a franchisee, go for it, but you shouldn't need this book to do so.

What would it mean for a creative business idea to reflect the uniqueness of its creators? Reflecting the uniqueness—the attributes of character, style, personality, and values—of the developer(s) of a business is paramount.

The way Richard Branson reimagines the businesses he creates under the Virgin brand—that somebody previously invented like the airline or mobile phone businesses—are examples of creative business ideas. Same for a new fashion business that mirrors the founder's image and her tastes, from the clothing type and style created, to the people she hires.

The terms *imaginative* and *original ideas* are deliberately chosen constraints designed to inspire you to strive for something out of the ordinary—a concept that reflects who you and your cofounders are as people.

Creative businesses of the kind I'm describing exist everywhere. For example, Reese Witherspoon, an active reader and book club fan, was reportedly not satisfied with roles for female actors, so she created her own production company—Hello Sunshine—to option movie rights for books with strong female characters.

The result? More roles for Reese and her fellow women actors, more books with strong female characters and female points of view turned into movies, and the creation of a thriving production/merchandising empire. Fantastic.

Witherspoon created a women-centered production company that focuses on women-centered stories. That was an original, or at least an imaginative, approach that reflected her personality and desire to fill an enduring void in the still male-dominated world of Hollywood.

Notice I'm not saying Hello Sunshine is an example of a creative business idea *because* it operates in a creative realm. I'm saying it's a creative business idea because it deployed original or imaginative ideas and is a reflection of who its creator is.

Creating a movie production house may not be for you, but there is a creative business idea that is right for you, and you alone.

Hayde López Rodríguez created Escuela Mexicana, an internationally recognized immersion Spanish language school in Guanajuato, Mexico, because of her passion for sharing Mexican culture, and because she felt her daughters would benefit by being around students from all over the world who would bring their cultures and perspectives to the school. Hayde says that marrying her motivations and her passions with her business means: "I can do what I love to do all day long and it feels like I'm not working."

Creative business ideas can flourish in any field from the life sciences, to music, to designer fashion or perfume, to entertainment, to creating a new franchise, and beyond. Publishing a book or creating a blog can be a creative business idea.

New forms for old ideas qualify and so can applying new business models to old businesses or adapting existing offerings to new markets. How about concepts that find ways to marry philanthropy with trade? Absolutely. Twists on a theme? Probably. Lots of those exist.

When Ray Kroc, now renowned burger baron, took the McDonald brothers' little restaurant nationwide, that was a creative business idea. According to *Entrepreneur,* the move to mechanize was reflective of Kroc's fascination with machinery. Through the McDonald's franchise, with its limited, branded menu, low prices, and innovative kitchen tech, such as a series of machines capable of producing forty milkshakes at a time, Kroc forged a new restaurant category: fast food.

Did McDonald's bring value to society at the time? That's a difficult question to answer, but an important one to ask. A better question: How is McDonald's bringing value to society today? Bringing value to society is a part of what makes a business idea creative.

A key hurdle aspiring entrepreneurs and existing business owners need to overcome in order to thrive today is ensuring that their business brings value to society. Asking the question and designing for a societal benefit will result in a creative flurry of innovative ways to add more value to society, *and* it will be good for your business. It's the new capitalism.

It's the capitalism of Blake Mycoskie, the founder of TOMS shoes (a certified B corporation) who created the One-for-One business model, meaning a pair of shoes is given away for every pair sold. As of 2019, TOMS had given away ninety-five million pairs of shoes. When the company expanded into eyewear and coffee, it expanded its giving model to match, restoring sight to three quarters of a million people, and bringing clean water to communities across the globe.

Does giving back get any better than that?

Creative business entrepreneurs might think of themselves as having a double bottom line or to be in pursuit of both purpose and profit goals, as Sonya Satveit, a Canadian MedTech entrepreneur and women's health advocate, puts it.

Creative business owners are more likely to seek B corporation certification that includes social and environmental performance and may see themselves eventually going public perhaps on Eric Ries's envisioned Long-Term Stock Exchange, an alternative exchange to Nasdaq and the NYSE, that holds companies to account for the creation of multiple stakeholder value over the long term, rather than shareholder value based on quarterly financial results.

Creative business ideas are all around us.

What kinds of businesses would *not* qualify as creative businesses? Many is the short answer, and this is not to denigrate any business form but rather to point out how they may not be CBIs.

A pizza shop that is part of a chain is not a creative business, for example. Individual chain restaurants in general are not creative business ideas, though the original concept for the franchise—to the extent it reflected the personality of the franchisor and deployed imaginative or original ideas—would be considered a creative business idea.

Could a consultancy be considered a creative business idea? Not usually, except when their services become packaged and branded or access to their services is done via a unique business model, or the service is aimed at a totally new market and the consultancy meets the other tests of a creative business idea.

Any business that does not deploy imaginative or original ideas reflecting its creator is not likely to be a creative business idea.

Here's the test. Does your business idea—

1. Deploy imaginative or original ideas?

2. Bring value to others (customers +), society, and to you, its creator(s)?

3. Uniquely reflect who you are?

If you answered yes to all three questions, yours is a creative business idea.

Tremendous benefits await you when developing a creative business idea from concept to reality.

- You will gain the satisfaction of seeing an offering that is a unique reflection of you and your cofounders and is valued by people in the world.

- Your business will stand out.

- You will be more likely to stick with your idea because it aligns with your values, interests, and desires.

- You may gain knowledge, esteem, and influence.

How would that be for a return on personal energy, imagination, and capital?

The timing to start a creative business has never been better. The advent of the internet, social media, blogs, design tools, e-commerce, person-to-person collaboration, and distribution platforms makes this an ideal time for creative business ideas to flourish.

My mission is to capture and share the essence of what creative business ideas are—and how to create them—with as many would-be entrepreneurs as possible. The embers are there. I want to fan the flame with a momentum-building way of getting there: the SPARK-CLICK-GO Journey.

Creative Business Idea Definition and Elaboration

A creative business idea (CBI) deploys imaginative, or original ideas, to deliver value for others and for society profitably, while uniquely reflecting and benefiting its creators.

CBI Components	Meaning	Elaboration
"A creative business idea (CBI) …"	An idea developed into a product, service, or creative production that has been tested and put out to the world plus business structures and processes to support it.	The goal of this book is to encourage readers to bring their ideas forward from concept through testing to reality.
"… deploys imaginative, or original ideas …"	Use of imaginative or original ideas helps a creative business idea to stand out or be set apart from common businesses.	Aspiring entrepreneurs stretch their thinking and ambition so they can bring something fresh to the world in an existing category or via creation of a new category.
"… to deliver value for others and for society …"	Users or customers gain either an economic, physical, or emotional benefit by using or experiencing your product or service. Society is improved.	Customers derive value that they alone determine in exchange for the price/fees paid. Having a societal benefit eliminates immoral businesses but includes environmental and positive quality-of-life benefits.
"… profitably …"	In order for it to be a business, there must be the potential for profit.	Works of charity would therefore be excluded, sadly, as would creative works done for yourself or pro bono.
"… while uniquely reflecting … its creators …"	Some aspects of the creator's character and values and what they want to see in the world must shine through in order to be a CBI.	This is what the creators uniquely bring to the world. The trick is creating something others value as an offering. SPARK-CLICK-GO is here to help.
"… while benefiting its creators."	The creators will gain in terms of recognition, reputation, influence, and knowledge.	Creating a business is hard work that can be done smartly and should be rewarding.

3
One Foot in Front of the Other

The SPARK-CLICK-GO Journey has been designed to

- Help aspiring entrepreneurs like you to come up with more and better ideas, and to select a promising idea to work on,
- Simplify the journey by breaking down the major component parts, and
- Show how an idea can be developed and tested as you progress toward bringing a new creative business idea to the world.

Taking an idea from initial spark through to building something, sharing it with people, and running with it is both a journey and a skill set you can learn and benefit from in predictable and unimagined ways.

First, what is SPARK-CLICK-GO and why am I calling it a journey?

The SPARK-CLICK-GO Journey is a process designed to help an aspiring entrepreneur build momentum by discovering, developing, testing, launching, and strengthening a creative business idea. I call it a journey because building a business is just that. Like any other journey there is a destination in mind and expectations associated with that destination.

To get to a physical destination—especially one you've never been to—a map or a GPS is helpful as is a method of transport, the skills associated with driving or maneuvering through transportation hubs, finding food and shelter, and resources in the form of money, energy, and time. For many journeys in life to be successful, a lot of people in supporting roles are needed. Think about the airline crew or road crews, for example.

For a creative business idea to become real, many of these same things are needed—namely, the right skills at the right time, resources, knowledge, and the collaborative efforts of others. Once you have a destination in mind, you'll need a road map, some tools, inspiration, and maybe some luck to get there. That's where SPARK-CLICK-GO comes in.

The phrase SPARK-CLICK-GO captures the three critical phases of the journey. I have broken down each phase to make clear what should be happening at that time.

SPARK is about discovering a need and developing a concept. CLICK is about designing, testing, and building your product, service, or creative production. GO is when you launch to the real world.

Here is how SPARK-CLICK-GO: A powerful journey looks in a diagram and a more detailed map of the journey follows:

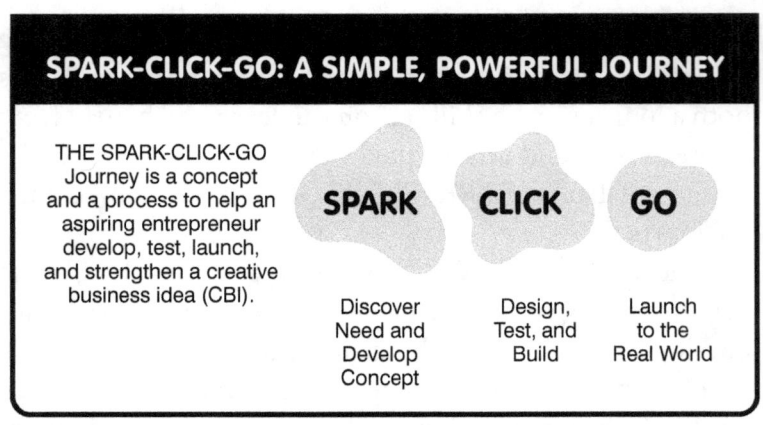

THREE PHASES OF THE SPARK-CLICK-GO JOURNEY

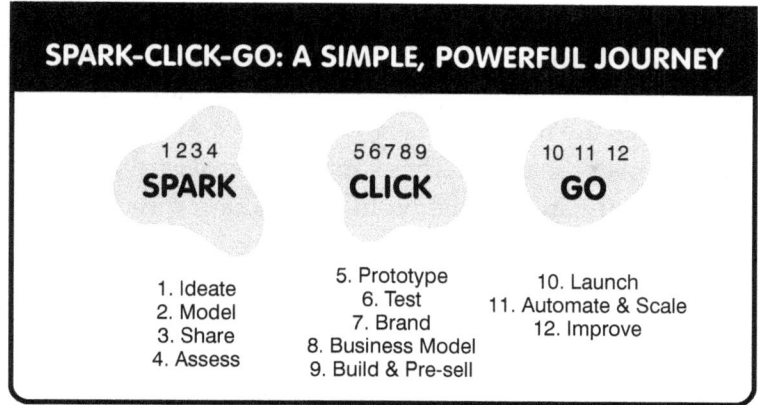

DETAILED COMPONENTS BY PHASE OF THE SPARK-CLICK-GO JOURNEY

Here's what you can expect to see and do along the route.

SPARK

Discovering a need is step one. Finding an idea—that's what trips up a lot of people. If you come across a need to address—a problem to solve—you have a chance of developing a solution. So the SPARK phase of the journey starts with need(s) discovery, but it doesn't end there. That's just the beginning.

A need, or a problem, is like a puzzle. There may be many ways to solve a puzzle or there may be no solutions—at least not until now.

If you have a solution in mind, start shaping it—start making a model of your concept. This is when you get out your sketch pad and you sketch. It's when you take a pen to paper, place your fingers on the keyboard, hop on Illustrator or Autodesk, or print a 3-D model.

Do whatever you need to do to wireframe your possible solution. Rough and nonfunctional is what you are aiming for. You want just enough shape so target users can pick up what you are laying down—and add to it. Once you have shaped your idea in some way, you can share it with others.

When I lived in the Bay Area in northern California, I collaborated with Brandon Cardwell the director of iGate, a local tech incubator, to organize and run two Startup Weekend events. Startup Weekends are competitive events that take place all over the world. These branded events are sponsored by the Kauffman Foundation in conjunction with Techstars. In forty-eight hours, contestants have to come up with an idea, form a team, shape a solution, and compete in front of judges.

Startup Weekends are like *America's Got Talent* for aspiring entrepreneurs. Picture thirty people, organized in seven or eight teams, feverishly working on ideas as diverse as a personal security app for smartphones, an online one-touch survey tool, or educational toys made from arduinos (simple open-source microcontrollers and software).

A drumbeat in the Startup Weekend format is to get participants out talking to potential users to explore needs and their teams' solution(s). This is a productive way to identify and validate unmet needs that could be fulfilled by the business solution a team is imagining.

Getting feedback from potential users can best be done if some shape is first given to the envisioned solution. So model your idea and start sharing your thinking.

Surface test your idea to find out whether your understanding of the problem, and your envisioned solution, resonates with your intended customers. If it does not resonate, adapt and try again. Restate the problem—make sure the problem is real and present for your intended customer. Do the same with your solution. Repeat until it resonates.

Once you've done some initial work, you will want to assess your idea. You'll want to ask yourself: Is my idea worthwhile? What skill sets do I need to build and test a solution? How will I make money, and will this business be large enough to return what I need? Is there enough juice in the orange to justify the squeeze?

CLICK

Okay, so you've done some work. You've come up with an idea, you've shaped and shared a potential solution, and you've asked the hard questions. You've done research, some soul searching, you have cofounders with skills that complement your own, and you've decided your idea is worthwhile. Congratulations.

You've spent little time, and little money, and you have experience working on a potential solution to a problem that needs solving with people who may become your partners in the cause.

That is a terrific return on your investment and it's part of the SPARK-CLICK-GO Journey—you spend money and energy in small amounts first, building up over time as your idea proves out and resonates with your intended audience.

Once you've decided your idea is worth building, you're ready to start working. You're entering the design, test, and build phase I call CLICK.

It's here you will build a prototype—an early version of your offering. You'll test it to see if it's working well functionally and to see if it's CLICKing with important audiences. You'll refine your solution and test again as many times as needed.

Did you know that Sir James Dyson built 5,126 prototypes over fifteen years before he created his namesake bagless vacuum cleaner? It's an inspiring feat demonstrating that perseverance and creativity in business can pay dividends. Dyson is both a billionaire and a knight.

If your prototype is functional—and not too ugly—you can start exploring ways to find customers. The key in the beginning is to find a small group that really likes your idea and is willing to try it out—warts and all. Tell them how much you are planning to charge for your offering and gauge their reaction.

All of this work is done before you go to the bigger step of designing a full-on production product, manufacturing line, or professional development of your service or creative production.

The CLICK phase of the journey is about building your offering and gaining *traction*.

Build-test-adapt. Build-test-adapt. Wash-rinse-repeat, as many times as needed.

You may get it right the first time—or your prototype might be right the ten-thousandth time, as it was for Thomas Edison with his lightbulb filament. Imagine. Trial then error. Trial then error. Nine thousand, nine hundred, ninety-nine times. My fingers are sore typing that.

Maybe you'll get it right early on and you can try to get a small group of users to try your product, and maybe you can even charge for it in the manner you had envisioned.

GO

Imagine that all goes well during the design and testing phase and you decide to build the market-ready offering. Your investment will be much more likely to succeed because of your early rounds of development and testing.

You are about to bring your creative business idea to the world. You're ready to launch. Excellent. Depending on the type of creative business idea you are working on, this could be a no-holds-barred affair, or it could be a low-key affair. If you created a movie, you will release it to as many theaters as possible. If it's software, you are—nowadays at least—capable of releasing it to the world.

I worked in Silicon Valley on a software start-up that allowed Airbnb hosts to set their nightly prices based on ever-shifting demand factors. The data pipe for the software-as-a-service to work was local, meaning we could only turn it on city by city. Conquering the world was going to be slow.

Hopefully, you will have some time to test your customer acquisition models prior to your main launch to find out what works. Maybe Facebook ads? Maybe Instagram? Maybe a blog you start will attract a lot of followers and drive them to your website. You're going to build a website, right? You'll want to figure out how to build in loyalty or some kind of lock-in, or a way to spread your offering virally. What's key is you'll want the cost of your new customer acquisition model to be less than the profit you make from your sales to that same customer.

When one of my sons was about five years old, he decided to sell lemonade on the sidewalk of our semi-urban home in Toronto one Saturday afternoon. Sales were brisk at fifty cents a cup, but when sales dipped, he changed the price to free, so I asked him:

"Why did you change your price to free?"

He said, "Because I will sell more."

To which I said, "Good point."

Volume up, yes, but at what cost?

SPARK-CLICK-GO is about building the right concept in the right way. It's about bringing a creative business idea to life—your creative business idea—one that resonates with customers and is a true reflection of you.

It's your journey.

My inspiration in creating SPARK-CLICK-GO is to help aspiring entrepreneurs like you to develop a worthwhile creative business idea. From there, profits will flow. It all starts with shaping a workable idea.

4

The Shape of Things to Come

If a picture tells a thousand words, how many words does a video convey? What about a model, or a blueprint, or a mock-up of the product you are conceiving?

Sonya Satveit is the CEO of a company called Qanik Dx whose mission is to bring home hormone testing to women. Her vision is to create an accurate, easy-to-use, one-step mini-lab for the home. Sonya and the team, whom I am helping out, are working to disrupt the usual routine: go to the doctor, get a lab requisition, go to the lab, wait for results.

Qanik's technology consists of a sensor and a cartridge with a test chip and receptors embedded within it necessary to detect human hormones using only a drop or two of blood.

Developing the technology, doing the clinical studies, and designing the manufacturing-ready devices and cartridges would require money, of course, so Sonya and one of her cofounders created slide decks to show interested parties and investors.

In the beginning, Sonya would describe the technology to interested parties, but people she was talking to did not always seem to understand what she was saying. She would describe the sensing device and the cartridges, but she was never sure what was being imagined by those she was talking with.

So Sonya and her cofounders decided to create a 3-D version of the device and started showing it to people especially when meeting them for the first time.

Now Sonya says, "The 3-D model creates an instant aha moment on calls with potential investors or partners—I think it helps others *imagine* what the actual production version will look like, and how it might work."

When Sonya shows the model to people, she can see in their eyes that they understand what she is trying to build, and they are much more able to absorb additional information about the company.

Creating a model serves as a useful representation of the product, service, or creative production you have in mind, and thus serves as a beacon to people wanting to help bring your idea to life. It's essential to give shape to your creative business idea. Here are some methods you can use. Some people start with sketching on a cocktail napkin. Some build elaborate models. The point is to put your idea into a form, or forms, helpful for sharing with others.

SHAPING YOUR CREATIVE BUSINESS IDEA

DIGITAL	BY HAND	DESIGN	PRESENTATION	MODEL
Illustration	Sketch	Blueprint	Elevator Pitch	Wireframe (UI)
Animation	Storyboard	User Experience	Perform	Architectural
Video	Caption/Vision	Graphic	Video	Financial
Slide Deck		Sets/Costumes		
Blueprint	**PROPOSAL**		**SAMPLE**	**CODE**
Storyboard	One-Pager		Product/Service	User Interface
Description	Query	**EXPERIMENT**	Chapter	Simulation
	Research	Protocol	Song/Scene	
	Project Plan	Abstract		

FORM FACTORS WITH WHICH TO SHAPE AND SHARE YOUR CREATIVE BUSINESS IDEA

Modeling is a critical step in moving your idea forward. Modeling is where you will start to shape a promising creative business idea, product, service, or production. It's where you express what you've been thinking since the SPARK of an idea hit you.

In this context, a model means anything that helps to capture the essence of your idea clearly and succinctly.

Depending on what field your business is in, standard models may be used to represent new ideas. For mobile software, a wireframe is often created to show what various screens of the user interface might look like. For advertising, a storyboard is created before an actual ad. A study protocol may be one of the first items you design if your business is in the scientific field—for example, a study to prove your concept.

I provide you with a menu of options in the accompanying diagrams to remind you of options you may already be aware of, and to stimulate your thinking to use a variety of forms. Maybe there is a new modeling approach you can work with.

The benefits of modeling your idea are many:

- Keeps costs low versus actually starting to build your offering

- Helps to focus and motivate you and your team

- Makes communicating with people external to your team easier

In another part of the book I talk about coming up with new ideas by "Uberizing" something. I heard this time and again when I worked with the start-up community in the Bay Area: "We're building the Uber for X," where X may be planes, trains, or rental vans or almost anything. It's annoying, it's overused, still, it's convenient shorthand, and it works as a model.

You can be creative by inserting any popular, successful business model and using it as an analog for your idea if appropriate.

"We're building the Tesla for trucking," for example, or "This is Etsy for biologists."

So using a short phrase, caption, or tag line is a kind of model that can quickly paint a picture in other people's minds of the idea you seek to bring to life. If people understand what your idea is using a short phrase, that is even better. If all you get are blank stares from people, you need to do more work.

I first became interested in Everbooked, the software-as-a-service (known as SaaS) company I became embedded with, when I heard what the team was working on: demand pricing for Airbnb hosts.

A useful exercise for capturing your idea in a bite-sized manner is the six-word challenge. I heard about it many years ago. I'm not sure who deserves the credit. The challenge is to capture the essence of your idea in only six words. Try it now. See what you come up with. For example: "Online home sharing and excursion marketplace" is a way to describe Airbnb.

Putting ideas into their simplest form is an art common to all forms: to writing, to biology, to mathematics, to logic, and to business.

An axiom I first picked up in California, in this case from Darren Buckner the CEO of Workfrom, was that useful software solves only one problem. A solid business—especially in the beginning—should solve only one main problem, too, and you can capture that essence with six words or fewer.

Giving your creative business idea a name can work in a similar way to distilling its essence to just six words. For me, coming up with a title for this book, *SPARK-CLICK-GO*, made clear to me what I wanted to create and share in a memorable way with people around me.

More helpful still was the subtitle, *How to Bring Your Creative Business Idea to Life*. The subtitle captured the substance of what I wanted to do and became the catchphrase or shorthand I used to explain what my book is about. A subtitle is to the actual title as a caption is to a cartoon or illustration—it adds meaning and color.

Naming my project helped me develop the book you hold in your hands, and it helped me communicate my idea to others. So give your creative business idea a project or working name.

A title communicates what is meaningful and memorable and ideally different about an idea. It's like a headline for a story in a newspaper or online news blurb—something that is meant to succinctly capture the essence of a longer piece, while grabbing the reader's attention. In the 1980s I came up with the name and a phone number for a delivery video service, 2-GO-VIDS. I enjoy coming up with titles for things.

Here's another way to capture the imagination of people. Come up with a clear and compelling vision for the idea you are working on. This too should be a short sentence or phrase.

Like the goal President Kennedy outlined to Congress in May of 1961 in the wake of Sputnik and Russian cosmonaut Yuri Gagarin's successful circling of the earth the month prior: "Before this decade is out, landing a man on the Moon and returning him safely to Earth." This is one of my favorite vision statements.

Americans rallied behind the idea including the janitor in the apocryphal story who, when asked years later what he did for NASA, said, "I'm helping put a man on the moon."

"A computer on every desk" is another compelling vision, as is "a world without Parkinson's disease."

What's common to vision statements such as these? Each evokes a picture of a desired future state and each stretches the reader's imagination. "Really," we might wonder, "how is that possible?" "They must know something we don't that gives them reason to believe in their goal." Or "Let's be sure to give them the support they need to make their vision a reality." All of these types of reactions contain energy—energy that might translate to support for your idea.

Let's pause for a moment.

When I write about giving shape to your idea, I mean modeling your product, service, or production (your offering) *and* the business that surrounds it.

In the beginning you may want to model out only your offering since that is often at the core of your creative business idea. If your idea is to take a well-known product or service and distribute it in a new way, then you should model your distribution model fully.

It can also be helpful to model your intended business model. The good news? You don't need to do both at one time and don't need to be comprehensive either.

For your business model, at this early SPARK phase, are you thinking fee-for-service, cost-plus, subscription, royalties, donations, or a printer and ink model, for example?

What other types of models might you create to help you show what your creative business idea is? If you are imagining a new store or franchise, you may want to sketch it first or have your drawings done professionally and show that around. To really get the point across, create a physical model of the store you are imagining using rudimentary craft materials or invest time with an architect to have a model created.

Sculpt your product idea if that is the best way to get across your idea, and you do not have access to a 3-D printer or the know-how to use one.

You can, of course, always write about your idea. For example, you might develop a detailed or a summary proposal of your intention. Or you can simply write about your idea in descriptive terms covering as many components of your idea you think your audience will be interested in.

If you are more comfortable creating a presentation deck instead of writing, then do that. If it helps you to think through your idea, communicate it, and get feedback, go for it.

If you're in software, you may want to use a prototyping tool such as Photoshop, Illustrator, or your favorite design program to draw up a user interface. Recognize that you'll need a whole lot more than that to create a working app, let alone a business.

Better than the use of a prototyping tool would be to do the actual coding required for your app—both the back end (database) component and the front end (user interface). You do not need to complete your app, but showing basic functionality can be very helpful for communicating your idea. And showing is better than telling as most software entrepreneurs know.

You can always work with a designer to come up with an early model of your offering.

You could animate your idea. I did this with a colleague when working for a company called Everbooked. We worked with an animation house to create a one-minute video animation about our business. The process forced us to come up with a succinct script describing what our business was, how it worked, and what the benefits were. It's amazing how few words fit into a short clip like this.

Once you have the video, you can post a link to your website or embed it in a presentation or pull it up anytime you want to explain what your business idea is.

Often these animations are used after your business is up and running, but why not invest a couple hundred bucks to create one early on in your development using it to inform and motivate people around you?

You could also storyboard your idea. This works well if your creative business idea is a video or live production but can also work well if you want to illustrate the behavior change your idea seeks to create among the audience. Imagine what a storyboard for Uber might have been (before it was Uber):

> FRAME 1: *Two friends outside of a bar looking a little disheveled.*
>
> Call-out: "Hey, how are we going to get home tonight?"
>
> FRAME 2: *Friend one, smartphone in hand, showing friend two.*
>
> Call-out: "Presto. Uber will be here in three minutes."
>
> FRAME 3: *The friends get in the car. One of them is waving as the car pulls off from the curb. The license plate of the car says UBR DRVR.*

See what I mean?

Can your new business idea be well told with a storyboard?

A video starts with a storyboard. Creating engaging videos takes a lot of work but may be worth it. You can use the storyboard you created earlier as a starting point or draw up a new one. Your script would be the result of thinking through the main elements of your business. It's a slow way for you to model your business, but it's a quick and rich way for people to see what your business idea is in action.

A pitch is a kind of storyboard that gets scripted and performed. As you may be aware, a lot has been written about pitches and pitching. So much so that it seems all you need for a strong business is a strong pitch. Here is my experience.

Developing a pitch is an essential part of moving forward with your business to attract founders, funders, or partners. As with many of the modeling methods mentioned in this chapter, the pitch forces you to think clearly and then communicate clearly about your idea.

I divide pitches into two types: funding pitches and everything else. Everything else can include pitching your business idea in a competitive forum.

At this early stage, you really only need an elevator pitch. The elevator pitch is similar to what you came up with during the six-word exercise. Assume you're working on a start-up in the entertainment business, and you have sixty seconds on an elevator or in the line at Starbucks with someone you've been trying to meet, what do you say?

You can definitely get your six-word description out. That will take care of the "what" your business is. Tick. It will probably also get your entertainment shark either interested, or her eyes will glaze over. If the latter happens, STOP. Get out of the elevator, or cafe, go home and work on your elevator pitch.

Assuming the first words out of your mouth created some interest and intrigue, your shark is now waiting to hear what is unique about your idea. She wants questions like these answered: Is your idea making waves now and with whom, and should I give this yahoo more of my time?

What do you do now?

You better get out the reason—the why—you are creating this business (to solve a major problem or tap into a unique insight, a new trend, or a burgeoning market) and something about your early success or your past success and what you are looking for in a partner.

The basic form is this: I have an idea that will solve a problem in your field, that will improve your bottom line by x or increase your growth by y.

On the subject of money, is a financial model necessary, and if so, when?

What you need to do is a basic calculation of your potential sales, less the unit cost to provide your product or service, to see how much you need to sell to cover your fixed costs and to make a profit. Identify the costs in your business such as how much it costs you to make your offering, salaries, commissions, manufacturing, inventory holding, selling, and distribution costs.

List your assumptions and then stand back and ask yourself if you can create the scenario you are imagining and whether it is worth your blood, sweat, and tears to get there.

To get to a forecast, do research to figure out your potential costs. Whenever estimating costs, take your best guess and then add 20 to 50 percent. At least. It's human nature to underestimate your costs and the time and effort you will need to dedicate to your business and to overestimate your sales and profits.

Effort you expend exploring the idea you are giving shape to will repay you doubly. As President Dwight D. Eisenhower is confirmed to have said in 1957: "Plans are worthless, but planning is everything."

What Eisenhower meant was the process of planning demands a thorough exploration of options within a specific context, and that the knowledge gained from the investigation will inform, but not necessarily dictate, future actions.

This chapter has been about creating a model of the product, service, or production that first came to you as a SPARK. Once you've created shareable bits or bytes that represent the promise and the possibilities of your creative business idea, you'll be much better equipped to share them with people in your circle, with confidants, partners, and the most important people of all, your future customers.

Reflect & Act

- The creative process in business, as in the arts and elsewhere, requires putting into form what the brain has conceived. The process of doing that is helpful for the person doing the creating and for the person or people who may be asked to comment on, change, critique, or add to the idea.

- What helpful forms can you express your creative business idea in and through?

- Where and with whom can you start sharing your idea?

5
Let's Talk

At this early stage in your journey, your first goal is to tighten up your understanding of the need you are filling—to better understand and define the problem you are going after. Your second goal is to develop your concept. Keep these two foundational goals in mind as you share your idea. You want to find out if the initial SPARK for your idea resonates with your intended audience.

Probe with potential customers to ensure you fully understand their needs. Keep asking why. Peel the onion. And when you show or describe the offering you have in mind, take a moment, be still, listen.

Consider these benefits of sharing your idea:

- Learn if your creative business idea is valued—and in which aspects specifically. Are you deploying imaginative or original ideas? Is this truly an expression of yourself—can you and your founders be *seen* in the execution of the idea presented? How will your offering benefit others? Are members of your intended audience receptive to the price you have in mind—the one at which you meet your profit needs?

- Understand who might become early customers.

- Pick up introductions to people who could help you with development, testing, or commercialization.

- Improve your ability to communicate your idea succinctly to people hearing about it for the first time.

- Gain valuable input into ways to improve your offering.

The natural tendency is to keep your idea secret until one day you open it up to the world—you come out of stealth mode—and the world embraces you and your idea. What a fantasy. This may be appropriate if you are working on something top secret, or something that could be readily copied, or done better quickly by a motivated third party, but not for most creative business ideas.

The truth is, ideas are plentiful, and what is plentiful is cheap. What *is* valuable are good ideas that mean something to founders like you who take the time to develop them—for people who build momentum via the SPARK-CLICK-GO Journey—not for people who think an idea is all you need to build a business.

What you don't want to give away when you share your idea is anything proprietary such as a specific methodology that you plan to patent, for example. And while you do need to be circumspect around some people—like another team who may be working to solve the same problem—being secretive can work against you.

Why is this?

Being secretive deprives you of the chance to gauge reaction, to learn if there is a need for your idea, to learn if there's an existing or upcoming solution to the same problem that may block yours before it launches.

The main reasons sharing your idea does not usually jeopardize you is that people either do not have the bandwidth, motivation, skills, resources, interest, or energy to steal your idea. Developing a business from idea to finished production on the market takes a lot of work and energy. Focusing on one promising idea is the way successful entrepreneurs win—it means forsaking all other ideas.

When you put your idea out into the world, you get to talk about it and, hopefully, you learn something valuable that will help you shape your idea into something more likely to resonate with the intended audience.

You have your collateral—the artifact(s) you created to represent your business idea. Now pick someone in your circle, someone with an open, positive mind, and invite them for coffee—or a virtual meeting—with the expressed purpose of talking about your idea. Done. Not so hard.

Now share your idea with someone in the customer group you are trying to appeal to or get a third-party researcher to share your idea on your behalf. When we were thinking of expanding our reach to smaller biotech companies, at the consultancy I've been associated with for many years, we created a suite of hypothetical offerings and took it directly to influencers at companies like the ones we wanted to eventually sell to so we could gauge their reaction.

The more you share your idea and your goals, the more you will likely realize most people just want to help. They don't want to steal your idea just as they don't want to be buttonholed and be made to feel obligated to sign up for your presale, but they will want to give their opinions on how to shape your idea.

You should share your idea as early as you feel appropriate. When your idea is really fresh, be sure to pick people to share your idea with who will receive it with an open mind and who are adept at building on an idea in a constructive manner. With every person you decide to approach, have a clear purpose in mind as to why you are approaching that particular person.

Choose your audience based on how far along you are in development of the idea. For example, if you have identified a clear need or problem, you may want to go to a designer who can work with the guide rails of a solution you give them. If you have a blueprint of a design already, you may want to share it with developers or engineers.

Years ago, I participated in a Startup Weekend event held at Impact Hub's open workspace in the Mission district in San Francisco—the Gothic-style building formerly inhabited by the *Chronicle*. During one of the scrums, when individuals and teams scour the floor looking for anyone to talk with about their business idea, I was cornered by two women who had an idea for a home-hairstyling business.

The first woman said, "Hey, what would you think of a home-hairstyling business?" I guess I looked a bit stunned.

The second woman said, "You'd simply put a request into an app on your phone, and someone would come to your apartment and cut your hair. You could even pay on the app."

"Would you use a service like this?" said woman one.

I said, "Hmmm, I'm not sure."

"Why not? Wouldn't it be great if you could just pick up your phone, press a couple buttons, and, presto, your stylist would be right over?"

"No, I don't think I would use the service," I said. "I'm not sure I'd be comfortable—I don't think it's for me."

The women left. They were looking for a confirmation, and when they didn't get one from me, they bailed. What a missed opportunity.

They didn't know what was running through my mind. They didn't ask me about my objections. They never found out that I lived outside the city and not in an apartment, that I spent next to nothing going to an old-style barber shop in the town I lived in, where I paid cash, that I would not want to nor would I feel comfortable having a woman come to my home to cut my hair. Not to mention the mess.

None of these quick thoughts are necessarily rational, but they were my thoughts, and it might have been useful to the two aspiring entrepreneurs to have explored my resistance a little more.

The job you have when sharing your idea is not to sell but to listen. The job is to figure out what's in the invisible thought bubbles hovering over someone's head as they are talking to you, and to understand. Maybe I wasn't the right customer, or maybe some of my concerns should be addressed as the eager pair develop their home-haircutting concept into a business.

It could turn out that this new delivery approach for hairstyling will become the next must-have, app-based, person-to-person service, and I will get over my concerns, as I did—and many of us did—with ride-sharing or renting an overnight room in someone's home. Or maybe not.

Make sure you share your idea with intended customers, especially the ones who seem open to trying new approaches to common problems. These people, sometimes classified as innovators, are the first group of folks likely to embrace new ideas in a given area. They don't walk around with a name badge that says "Innovator," nor do they sport "Early Adopter" hats, or "Early or Late Majority" or "Laggard." You have to find these people.

You'll know who the innovators are by the media they frequent or subscribe to, where they work, perhaps what similar latest gadgets they have purchased, by their websites and social media profiles, by their response to online or physical ads you place seeking people interested in the latest x, y, or z. They are worth finding because they will be eager to work with you if you bring them something new to play with.

Sharing your idea with experts can also be worthwhile since they have their fingers on the pulse of the market and they know the tricks of their trade. These folks are not necessarily innovators, but they make it their job to know everything that's happening in the space. Just be wary, they may also be the ones to tell you something can't work, that they've seen it all before. Don't get discouraged—find an expert, or more than one, and get them into your corner.

Look to Friends and Family for Support

You want friends and family to know what you are doing. So unless you think they will mock, discourage, or resent you, then share your idea. Friends and family members can offer you moral support plus food, water, and shelter while you toil away on your idea. But be cautious when receiving praise. There has never been a mother who thought her baby was ugly, or at least never one who said so aloud. Your closest friends and family members are not going to tell you your baby is ugly either, even if it is.

When I shared with my friends and family the journey I was on to research, develop, and write this book, they generally said, "Wow, that's great, good luck." Some offered to help. I was appreciative of their love and support, of course, and I hope you have supportive people in your life, but for your business to CLICK, you are going to need input from your customers and key people within the ecosystem you will be operating in.

Share your idea with your spouse or a friend close to you, and just be clear with them who the intended audience is and what you are trying to accomplish. With friends and family your goal is not to get feedback on whether they would use your service. Rather, you are seeking an opinion on whether the idea makes sense given the facts you present to them. If your confidant has a flair or knowledge in a particular field, for example, design, ask for their opinion on design.

With your closest family members, spouse, or significant other, you will probably want to sketch out the time commitment, finances, and lifestyle changes you think you will need to develop and launch the business idea you have in mind. You will need the support.

Is that a Demo in Your Pocket?

When I moved with my family in 2012 to the Bay Area and I decided to focus more of my career with start-ups, it became clear to me that everyone had a start-up idea or at least a pet project they were working on.

Did you see the TV comedy series *Silicon Valley* by Mike Judge? It's a satirical take on Silicon Valley. I remember the first season of the show—maybe during the first episode—when one of the characters, probably the main one, new to the Valley, goes to what looked to me like the Stanford hospital to see a doctor. The doctor takes care of our protagonist's (his patient's) health concern, and before the two of them exit the examining room, the doctor is demonstrating an idea he's working on for a new health app, or medical device.

This is exactly how I remember the Valley—everyone has a mock-up of an app or designs of something they're working on in their pocket, ready to be drawn faster than Billy the Kid's pistol. Silicon Valley has its own culture.

I'm not suggesting this is bad. On the contrary, I found the mindset in California refreshing. The status quo was not the driving philosophy—finding a better way of doing things or heading out to change the world keeps the wheels turning in the minds of people there. Ongoing vibrations of the Gold Rush, too, are alive and well—everyone is rushing to find their fortune panning for yellow minerals in the streams of the new Sierra.

Many places are available to you to share your idea. ABS—always be sharing—is not a bad mantra, but just make sure you whip out your mock-up to the right people, for the right reasons as often as you show it to the kid at the grocery store bagging your groceries.

The best place is where your potential customers are, for example:

- In situ (that is, where they hang out or do their work—in their habitat)
- At an exhibit or showcase you create
- At a convention
- At a focus group
- At a one-on-one interview

Additional places to share your idea include these:

- On the street—hopefully on a block where future customers pass by
- At a meetup
- At a pitch competition
- In an investor's office
- At an accelerator or shared workspace for start-ups
- At a class
- On *Shark Tank* (if you can get on, odds are about 1 in 400)
- At a theater

And online here:

- On a landing page
- On your social media pages
- On a testing portal
- On a call-in/text-in show
- On your own website
- At a virtual meeting
- Via email

Share your offering with people from different vantage points. The most important audience usually are the intended customers since they are the people who will pay for your offering—they are the ultimate arbiters.

Be clear about whose perspective you are gaining as you share your idea, and what it means for your venture.

I will discuss the different perspectives in greater detail elsewhere in the book. For now, let's say you have customers, tech people, money people, your fellow creators, influencers, and cheerleaders.

Here are a couple of examples of sharing an early idea—maybe just the SPARK of an idea, or a preliminary description—to see how it resonates.

Let's revisit Startup Weekend for a moment to see what kinds of forums they create for people to bring their ideas to the crowd. Aspiring entrepreneurs who come to Startup Weekend are encouraged to come to the weekend event prepared to pitch an idea that others might work on. The purpose is to surface the ideas that the group has the most energy for.

Picture a room full of eager participants craning to hear your pitch—pizza and Cokes in their hands. You have one minute to both describe your idea and gain the interest of those participants.

After the rapid pitch round, the ideas are posted on the wall, and participants walk around the room to learn more about the idea from the person who pitched it. It's stiff competition. Any idea that is supported by a minimum number of participants (which might be just one additional person) is chosen as an idea to be worked on for the weekend.

As an aspiring entrepreneur with an idea, you have to be clear and compelling in your pitch. In this case you are pitching to fellow creators who need to decide how they will spend their time for the weekend. In part those fellow creators have their customer hat on, too, thinking to themselves: "Is this product or service this person is envisioning something I might potentially use or could see others using?"

What Problem Are You Solving?

Be clear about the problem you are solving. As Jake Mendel, a Silicon Valley start-up banker, writes on Medium, the key question to ask yourself is this: "What problem are you solving?"

He suggests that first time founders normally respond by launching into a five-minute diatribe about an amazing opportunity or disruptive technology—yet often they'll miss answering the question all together. Veteran founders provide a problem statement.

- What is the problem?
- Who has this problem?
- Why is it a problem?"

A problem statement may include some time boundaries and a quantification of the magnitude of the problem, but it is essentially human in perspective and in richness—it's about empathy and clarity.

So spend some time to understand the unmet need from the perspective of your intended customers' viewpoints. Put yourself in their shoes. Understand what they do now, what they wish they could do, and how they feel about the problem.

Sharing your potential solution with intended customers will help to surface unmet needs they have and will ignite conversations around your intended solution and how to adapt it.

An Example from Book Publishing

Reedsy is a two-sided marketplace platform where authors go to find editors, designers, and marketing support people to help turn their creative ideas into reality. For editors and other independent contractors, it is a place to find gigs.

One interesting event Reedsy sponsors online is called *First Line Frenzy* featuring professional editor Rebecca Heyman. During the event, callers offer up the first line of a novel or work of nonfiction in progress. Heyman listens to the opening lines, asks a question or two of the author calling in, may banter a bit with the host of the web meeting, and then gives her expert opinion to the caller.

Heyman tells the audience whether the opening line works or does not work, what she recommends to improve it, and sometimes gives her emotional reaction. The sessions are dynamic and interesting for the audience, and especially to the authors submitting their work.

What's important for the folks with the creative (business) ideas to realize is that the feedback is from an expert, but only one expert, in their field. Heyman may or may not represent (probably not) their intended audience, nor is she trying to. She is looking at the submitted work in the context of the category (the genre) and from the perspective of an editor with a wealth of experience in the publishing arena. The first line sets a tone and is meant to create interest in what follows, so it's important to the book—just as a brand and a tag line are tasked with doing for other businesses.

Therefore, take any feedback you receive in context. Try not to imbue opinion from any one person as gospel or as rubbish, unless it is from your sole intended customer.

You may be embarrassed now because the product you are hoping to create is perhaps not elegant. Maybe it is only described in profile in a document on paper or in a series of illustrations. It's not a real product yet—it doesn't *do* anything. It's inert. So what? Remember the reasons you are sharing your work. You need to get a feel for whether the seed you are carrying might land on fertile ground.

Compare the feeling you anticipate by sharing it now, and face the feelings you might experience, rather than sharing it later. A rejection now, or worse, disinterest, is much less painful than rejection later after you've poured a bigger part of yourself into your project.

SPARK—Need Discovery and Concept Development

The SPARK phase is all about igniting your offering by focusing on the needs of your intended customers and adapting your concept until it resonates with them. Here's a trial-and-error sequence to follow.

S-P-A-R-K
S = Solution
P = Problem
A = Adapt
R = Resonates
K = Keep

Start with your solution to the problem you are trying to solve and test it. If it resonates with your target customer and other essential players (more on who these folks are later), you are set to keep going. If not, adapt your solution or restate your understanding of the problem, and try again.

SPARK is about need discovery and concept development.

What is your exit pass from the SPARK phase? Being able to clearly state the problem you are seeking to solve in a few words and describing your intended solution with equal panache will earn you an exit pass from the SPARK phase.

You will likely gain much more by sharing your idea at an early stage than you risk by holding your idea in stealth mode. Be choiceful with whom you share your idea and frame the type of feedback you are seeking clearly. The risks of theft of your idea can be minimized by not revealing methods like details of any patents.

If your idea is truly reflective of you, by definition it cannot be copied—at least not the way you would do it—since you are unique. Sharing your creative business idea will help you to refine your idea, gauge its desirability, see blind spots, and may even lead you to some helpful people to bring along with you on your journey.

Now you have to decide if your idea is worth building. If your (adapted) solution resonates with customers, and it is a creative business idea that excites and makes sense for you, you're on the right track. But there's more to consider when deciding if your idea is worthwhile.

Reflect & Act

- Be deliberate about sharing your idea. Be clear about what you will share, with whom, where, and how you will share it, and what your goals are. Make sure your goals include a check on whether your idea meets the definition of a creative business idea and, if not, how it could be made more so.

- Sketch out a description of the people you wish to share your idea with and figure out where members of your intended audience are and how to reach them. Decide who will do the research and make a plan to get out and do it.

- Developing a creative business idea is an iterative process. Think of it as homing in on a target. When you share your intended solution, it may, on first pass, miss the mark. Keep your reconnaissance efforts high to understand the root of the problem until you can clearly and succinctly state what the problem is, who has the problem, and why it is a problem. Being crystal clear about the problem you are solving is essential to creating and adapting a good solution—as essential as a clear diagnosis is to treatment selection.

6
What's Your Problem?

Let's take stock.

Creative business ideas unto themselves are not valuable until you start to give them shape and put them to the test. You have immersed yourself in the many ways to model your creative business idea, to give it shape. But how do you know your idea is exemplary?

Think of it this way: Creating a business takes up a lot of time. If all of your time is taken up creating your business, why not pick something likely to succeed? You can't work harder than "all the time," right? If you're going to work hard to build a reputation, why not build that reputation in a profitable area that you are passionate about?

While there is no such thing as a perfect idea—and there is certainly no magic way to predict whether a promising idea will do well in the marketplace—there are elements that make up a solid idea, and there are known pitfalls to avoid.

I want you to benefit from my thinking and experience in this area, to apply it to your idea(s), and to consider what my experiences may mean for you. But that's all.

The way to find out if you have an excellent idea is to build it and put it out to the real world. I'm just trying to increase your odds of success.

You may be wondering whether to model your idea and then assess it or assess it first. That is up to you, as is everything for an aspiring entrepreneur. Either sequence can work.

Many of the models I suggested to help shape your idea are easy and inexpensive, demanding little time and expense. Take the six-word challenge, for example. You could easily use that exercise, through which you develop a six-word sentence describing your idea, as a starting point for the assessment. If you have more than one idea, having each expressed with a short caption can be a handy way to keep each straight and to work with them.

Rockin' in the Free World

Let's look at an example. It's 2012 and Neil Young is out to give the free world music the way it sounded when it was made. The man has been making music for fifty years. He is an icon. He's the *Young* in Crosby, Stills, Nash & Young. He's a face on the Mount Rushmore of rock music.

Now he's out to save the world from poor sounding music files. And he's ticked.

He thinks compressed music files, played back on iPods and iTunes, means we are all listening to low-quality music, so he is on a mission to give us—the people—the kind of listening experiences we deserve. The kind of sound he has been recording with the more than thirty solo albums he has crafted.

It's an admirable mission.

Young's PonoPlayer is conceived as a high-fidelity stand-alone music player—one that will bring the listener into the recording studio to enjoy the music the way it was recorded by the artist. *Pono*, the brand name, is Hawaiian for righteous and pure.

Fighting for the right of fans to hear music the way it was recorded is a mission in keeping with Young's high standards and his legendary persona in music and culture. The PonoPlayer is a great product idea to stem the tide of poor quality music playback.

But is the PonoPlayer a promising business idea, and how does Young know this before he pours his blood, sweat, and tears into the endeavor?

Is Your Idea Strong?

In assessing whether your idea, like Neil Young's, is promising, the first question I implore you to ask is whether your idea meets the definition of a creative business idea. If it does, you should be well on your way to success. The reason? By definition your idea deploys imaginative or original ideas that bring value to others and is a reflection of you and your fellow founders. It has to have the potential for profit; otherwise, it is not a business, but that level of profit is defined by you—at least until and if you bring in outside investors.

So the anatomy of a promising idea includes meeting the definition of a creative business idea. When assessing whether an idea is promising, look both from an outside-in perspective and an inside-out vantage point. Both perspectives include elements of what makes a creative business idea.

Internal Factors of a Promising Idea

- Deploys imaginative or original ideas
- Is a unique reflection of you and your founders
- Poses exciting key challenges and acceptable risks
- Is an idea you and your team are well positioned to bring to life
- Has sufficient potential for return on effort/capital

External Factors of a Promising Idea

- Is valued by customers and meets the key need(s) of customers—solves a pressing, long-standing, or underlying problem

- Adds value for society

- Offers exciting key challenges with acceptable risks

- Gets people in your ecosystem to say things like, "You're onto something"

- Feels like the right timing

Use the following tool to help you assess your idea.

Idea Assessment Tool

Feel free to use check marks or a rating score from 1 to 5 for each criterion in the Idea Assessment Tool. You can use this to assess one idea, or more than one idea. Your idea should meet the definition of a creative business idea. (As a reminder: A creative business idea (CBI) deploys imaginative, or original ideas, to deliver value for others and for society profitably, while uniquely reflecting and benefiting its creators.)

If it does not, ask yourself what you can do to make it more so, or what shortcoming you can live with.

IDEA ASSESSMENT TOOL	
Internal and External Factors	**Answer Yes/No or Rank on a Five-Point Scale**
Idea meets the definition of a creative business idea.	
Idea meets the key need(s) of customers.	
Key challenges and risks identified are exciting and acceptable.	
Timing is good.	
You and your team are the right people to execute this idea.	
Idea has sufficient potential return on effort / capital.	
People say things like, "You're onto something."	
Add up the number of Yes answers or Total Points.	

Deploying original or imaginative ideas is not meant to be a bar that only a person with Herculean strength or Einsteinian intellect can surmount, as mentioned earlier. It is intended to get aspiring entrepreneurs like you to stretch your thinking and your ambition so you can bring something fresh to the world in an existing category or to create a new category.

You **Might** Be onto Something

How do you know whether your idea is strong? Let me take a Jeff Foxworthy approach:

- If your creative business idea meets a need that nobody else is satisfying, you *might* be onto something.
- If you have reliable long-term sources of inputs at low cost and can sell at a high price, you *might* be onto something.

- If key players in the field or potential customers say stuff to you like "Keep going" or "We could sure use that," you *might* be onto something.

- What if they say, "You *might* be onto something"? Well, hmmm, duh, you *might* be onto something.

- If you and your team are uniquely suited to develop this idea, you *might* be onto something.

- If something has changed in the market or there is new technology that you can deploy first or in an imaginative way, you *might* be onto something.

- If it is not likely that a big fish can swallow you up by duplicating your offering or you just know you can do better, you *might* be onto something.

- If the number of potential users is large or growing or underserved, you *might* be onto something.

- If there is potential for a strong return on your blood, sweat, and fears, you *might* be onto something.

- If you've shown a constant interest in this field and the solution uniquely reflects you and your team, you *might* be onto something.

- And to wrap up: If the key challenges are exciting and/or the risks are acceptable, you *might* be onto something.

Perry Chen, one of the Kickstarter founders, told Guy Raz, during an interview on the podcast *How I Built This,* he turns a new business idea over and over and upside down and sideways and over again. If it has a fatal flaw, he abandons it. In the case of Kickstarter, he couldn't find a fatal flaw, so he decided—along with two cofounders—to pursue his idea. Eight years later (don't ask) they brought Kickstarter to the world.

I love the idea of turning a new business idea over and over before committing to it. That search implies looking at the business idea from multiple angles. Should you discover a challenge that does not excite you or an unacceptable risk, you can then change or abandon that idea.

What's an example of a challenge that does not excite you or a risk that is not acceptable?

I suppose that is up to each of us to decide, but a challenge I saw countless times in Silicon Valley was the risk that an entrepreneur's idea could become a feature or business line of a larger competitor. A photo storage and sharing site was a wonderful idea until the behemoths Google, Apple, and Amazon started providing the same services. This continues to happen all the time.

Read the following list of challenges:

- Your technical solution is not possible (think, "beam me up, Scotty").

- You do not have the skills, or the resources to gain the skills, necessary to build your offering.

- The cost structure in the business means it may not become profitable (this is a key problem in scaling businesses requiring lots of customization such as craft furniture building).

- You do not have access to sufficient funding to get you to the next stage (this is a ubiquitous problem; the best thing to do is keep iterating until your solution resonates with customers and other key groups like opinion makers).

- You lack access to a key input (data or raw material) or a key input is expensive (like access to proprietary data or a supply of raw materials such as nuclear waste).

- Liability costs are high (like in the skydiving business; get lawyers involved to shift responsibility to users and search for insurers that understand your business and who may offer targeted insurance products to meet your needs).

- The success of your idea is critically dependent on something out of your control, like the climate.

- You do not have the freedom to operate from an intellectual property perspective (for example, you could step on someone else's patents) or you lack sufficient patents to protect yourself.

- Customers do not have the money to pay even if the value to them is there (example: solar panels in the early days).

- An entrenched competitor can squash you by replicating your idea (Apple now offers scanning capabilities on their phones so if your business is an app that provides the same, such as the excellent Genius Fax, you will need to keep innovating).

- The idea is currently illegal (take this for a spin: think about the legality of the ride/home sharing app businesses when they were starting out, and still to this day depending on the place).

- The market is small, declining, or crowded (sadly this is the case in many cities in the restaurant, tourism, and hospitality businesses during late 2020).

- Your idea is not different enough to be noticed in a crowded field.

Now reread the list. Do any of these challenges seem to fit your situation? If so, is your gut reaction excitement about overcoming the challenge, or dread?

A Rookie Mistake

It's the spring of 1995. My colleagues and I at a company called Knoll Pharma have spent the past few months assessing a product in our portfolio that we think might merit investment because of changing customer needs.

We excitedly share our findings at a portfolio meeting with our CEO, Al, who has to green-light funding of all products.

Al: "Looks like doctors might embrace a product like this. I like the cost of goods and the margin opportunities. It might be a stretch, but it would be doable to hire some new reps to promote it with some tweaks on the management side. How much patent life have we got left?"

Me: "Right. Thanks, Al. I'm glad you see it as a good opportunity. Let me look into that last question—the one about the patent—and get back to you."

Al: "Okay, sounds good, Doug. Next."

So I leave the meeting, tail between my legs, feeling dumb for not knowing the answer about the patent, and dumber for not having asked the question myself at the beginning of our quest.

I hustle over to a colleague's office and quickly discover the product has just over a year and a half remaining on its patent.

Talk about *Dumb and Dumber*.

I inform Al, our CEO, about the patent runway, and we agree to stop assessing the product further.

Luckily it was Al who asked the question about the patent, so he felt smart for asking it, and since he didn't realize how much work my team and I had put into the assessment, he really didn't perceive a loss.

The lesson I learned that day about the importance of probing for risks has stayed with me regardless of whether I'm assessing a new idea, working with an early-stage company, or interacting with a business unit of a large enterprise.

Patents are essential in pharma but may not be important or may not be relevant in your industry. But every business idea faces possible challenges and risks—lack of a runway from the protection of a patent or lack of freedom to operate because of your intellectual property situation is but one category.

Timing is another category of challenge and risk. Timing for this product idea seemed perfect when we looked at changing customer needs, but terrible when we looked at our patent runway. In comedy, they say timing is everything. They could say that about business too.

But if a challenge excites you and the risk is acceptable, that is a good sign you may be the right person to tackle the problem. This is where you could make your mark.

The Medium Is the Message

Picture this.

I'm in a coffee shop in New Jersey minding my own business. The year is 2008, maybe 2009. This guy is sitting at the table next to me. He looks a bit disheveled. He has a notebook in his hand and some coffee. It appears he's been here for most of the morning. He seems a little bit inside his own mind.

After a while he kinda just starts talking and tells me that he couldn't understand why we (society) didn't just have computer servers running programs that would be remote from our devices. He couldn't understand why we all bought computers and loaded applications and virus programs onto them. Why we did it this way at home and why companies paid for people to manage software on each computer, including loading programs, trouble shooting, and the like, seemed backward to him.

"Why," he asked (I think to me), "why can't we just do all these things remotely?"

"Think of it," he said, "nobody would have to physically load programs and take care of maintenance and viruses on their own machines. Wouldn't that be easier?"

I said, "Yes, I think so. That does sound like a good idea."

Turns out, that guy I met in a coffee shop in New Jersey was quite prescient. He basically predicted the advent of cloud-based software. I just wasn't sure he had any intention of pursuing the idea, whether he had the talent to do so on his own, or whether he could attract others to his vision—to help make it happen. From all appearances, he was just a guy with an idea—and a rant.

An insightful idea is a terrific start. Marry that idea with a talented and resourceful team who can build it, now you have something powerful.

How Do You Know If You Have a Good Idea?

I hope the criteria for what makes for a promising idea, as told in these sometimes humorous stories, help you identify the overall strength of your idea and where the gaps are.

Assessing more than one idea? Checking them against the hurdles identified may help you select the best idea to pursue or, if none of the ideas seem strong, may send you back to the starting point.

Deciding if your idea is worth building is essential to your sanity.

	IDEA 1	IDEA 2	IDEA 3
IDEA ASSESSMENT / SELECTION TOOL			
HURDLE A	✓	✓	
HURDLE B			✓
HURDLE C		✓	

IF YOU HAVE MORE THAN ONE IDEA, COMPARE THEM AGAINST EACH OTHER.

Look. Your lifeblood, your energy, what you uniquely bring to the world when you are at your best is a valuable commodity. You want to make sure to spend that capital on the right creative business idea.

If you find your idea to be lacking in overall strength, you might want to toss it out. That would be painful, I know. That pain, though, might be dwarfed when compared to the pain and regret you may experience if you pour yourself into an idea with an unacceptable risk.

Unless the risk you imagined was not borne out in testing or you can address that risk by rethinking your concept, it may be best to kill it. But if it's really just a super tough puzzle to solve, and the *solving* will bring a windfall, then get *solvin'*.

If your idea is deficient in one area, ask yourself how you might address that weakness or whether you can live with the likely outcome from that weakness. For example, if the weakness is in a particular talent area, you might be able to find a solution. If the audience you intended for your offering cannot and will not ever be able to afford your solution at a profitable level, see if you can push out costs by simplifying your offering. If the idea is not a reflection of you as an individual, or your founding team, ask yourself what changes you should make.

Advertising Is Eating the World

Let me take you back in time to an example. Would you have known AdWords was a worthy idea if you were in the room where it happened with Sal Kalmangar?

AdWords is Google's platform to sell keywords to advertisers—words or terms that are used by people searching to find what they are looking for online. In the beginning the concept was a radical departure for Google and the idea carried many risks.

If AdWords were my idea, here is how I may have assessed it. Attempting to be objective, I would have marked it of moderate to strong attraction. I probably would have given the idea high marks for Google's ability technically and from a funding perspective to pull it off and for proprietary access to a key input, data. I would have rated as attractive the potential revenue source.

My concern would have been whether the idea fit with the company's values, which were, at least looking from the outside, about a free and open internet and access to information.

So overall it looked like a moderate to strong idea, but I would have wondered if bringing advertising to a user's search experience represented an unacceptable risk.

What happened? The short story is they tested the idea with sample users and proved the concerns raised about turning off their users were massively overblown. As Mark Twain may have said, "I have had a lot of worries in my life, most of which never happened."

Search the web—Google—for more of Sal Kalmangar's story about the creation of Google AdWords. I have imagined some of it, but it is firmly based on information publicly available. AdWords went on to drive Google—now Alphabet's—revenue. So it turned out to be a stellar idea.

Go figure. And go test out your concerns.

In contrast, what's it like developing a bad idea? You get to do just as much work, expend just as much energy, but the gains do not tip the seesaw in return.

Had Neil Young assessed his PonoPlayer thoroughly, he may have realized his idea was aimed at needs not shared by a majority of the audience for MP3 recorded music, that the timing was not right for an audiophile's tastes on playback file formats, that people were looking mainly to replace their CD libraries with music they loved, and that convenience was a driving factor. Young and his team may have realized they were not the best people to champion an idea like the PonoPlayer.

What is the lesson? Assess your ideas at any stage to gauge their overall strength, to highlight weaknesses, and to figure out what would need to change for you to pursue them with vigor.

Use this approach and find or adapt a creative business idea worth building.

Reflect & Act

- Think about and be clear on the need you are aiming to satisfy—on what the problem is you are seeking to solve. Knowing the need you are aiming to address is as essential as knowing whom you are solving it for.

- If your idea meets the definition of a creative business idea, you are well on your way to choosing an idea worth building. Determine whether you have the right team and the resources to pursue this idea and, if not, figure out what is needed to change that.

- Are there ways to make your idea better fit the definition of a creative business idea? If not, make sure you can live with the shortcomings. Do the challenges you see excite you and are the risks acceptable to you? If not, give serious thought to killing your idea—to failing fast.

7
A Work in Progress

Alli Webb was living in the Brentwood area of LA when she ventured out of her job as full-time mom and into the hairstyling hall of fame. Okay, you might not find a hairstyling hall of fame on a map, and Webb and her cofounders did not walk into a building that doesn't exist.

But Alli and company were not just blowing hot air when they created a new category in the styling world. And it all started with the SPARK of an idea that moms like her might want and be willing to pay for—blowouts delivered to their homes.

As Webb, a trained hairstylist with roots in the New York salon world, told host Guy Raz of the *How I Built This* podcast, she had been musing about starting a mobile hairstyling business (SPARK), so she posted her potential offering on Peachhead, a Yahoo group with about five thousand moms as members.

Her posting went something like this:

I'm a professional stylist thinking of offering a blowout styling service for moms in their homes. I'm thinking of charging thirty-five or forty bucks. Interested? Pls contact me.

She was flooded with responses. CLICK.

And so began her mobile blowout service called Straight at Home that was the prototype of what would become

Drybar, a business that has employed some three thousand stylists in more than seventy stores reaching $100M in revenues. Alli Webb's business is a terrific example of a creative business idea.

Some of the elements from those early days—like facing the client away from a mirror so she could be spun around for the big reveal—became design elements for her first and subsequent stores as did the pricing she started with which she had picked for Straight at Home because two twenties "was just easy."

Of course, her mobile service was personal as well, creating a bond between stylist and client in some cases. These were among the early elements that started a pattern—a prototype—for the first Drybar salon and subsequent franchises that she, her husband, and brother would go on to create.

By creating a working prototype that allowed her to test customers' reactions to her service, Alli was able to gain a key insight—that there was a big hole in the current market. Her customers told her that in situations when Alli was unavailable to do their blowouts, they went to their regular salons, got overcharged for the service, and felt pressured for not getting a full cut, or they went to a discount place down the street.

Webb saw this as a choice between two bad alternatives and designed to fill the middle with a salon focused exclusively on blowouts. Her brick-and-mortar solution solved a key fault she discovered in her mobile model—all her profits went out the tailpipe in fumes.

Prototypes are not just for products invented in labs or by engineers.

"HAVE BLOW DRYER, WILL TRAVEL."

Test. Learn. Test.

Let's say you want to open a new business. What's a better approach? Go all-in, invest in a new plant, spend hundreds of thousands on a new store, buy a ton of inventory, or test the water first?

Small steps.
Small investment.
Big returns.

If your early version doesn't catch on, regroup or bail out.

A prototype is a first model of your creative business idea, product, service, or production. It sets the pattern for the offering you are creating.

This is one of the first opportunities for you to test the original or creative ideas you are deploying. It's an essential element of the SPARK-CLICK-GO Journey. Before releasing to the real world—test. Learn. Test again.

We humans love patterns. We get attached. That's why we need to remain open to user feedback as we develop and test early versions of our offerings.

When you hear or see the word *prototype*, what pops to mind? Edison's lightbulb and the ten thousand materials he tested as filaments before he found one that worked, or maybe Dyson's bagless vacuum cleaner in a workshop strewn with vacuum cleaner entrails? Is the image popping into your mind an invention? I'm guessing the scene you are conjuring is a studio, lab, or workshop.

Whatever it is you are imagining is fine (it's your imagination), but did you know that virtually all would-be entrepreneurs have the opportunity to create a prototype even if it's for a service or a production? You may not hear the term *prototype* in your field because a different term is used, but prototypes can be found—early and prerelease versions and perhaps many versions in between—in every new business.

Here are some of the many reasons to develop a prototype of your creative business idea or offering:

- To see if it works
- To prove that it works
- To ID blind spots and adapt your technology
- To gauge emotional reactions
- To test for ease of use
- To determine which application your solution may be best suited for
- To earn additional investment

Building a prototype makes your idea real. It proves that you and your team are capable of building something that works and possibly works better than other solutions addressing a similar problem. A 3-D model is to a working version of your offering as water is to wine. Going from a sketch on a napkin to a working early version of your idea is like turning Pinocchio into a real boy.

The podcasting entrepreneur John Lee Dumas wanted to create a service that would help interested parties become expert podcasters. He knew there was interest in this idea because members of his podcast, *Entrepreneur on Fire*, kept hitting him up for advice. SPARK.

What did John do? In 2013, according to his website, John started a service called PodPlatform. "The vision for PodPlatform was that podcasters would record their episode, upload it to PodPlatform, and then John would edit and upload the episode to Libsyn." The only problem—it did not CLICK with his audience.

John hadn't created a prototype of PodPlatform and hadn't tested it. Instead of simply accepting this failure, John dug in with members of his audience—*Fire Nation*—who were interested in podcasting and started talking with them one-on-one to find out their biggest struggles. That's when he came up with the idea to create Podcasters' Paradise, an online membership and community teaching individuals how to create, grow, and monetize their own podcast, according to his website.

After working on the basic elements of Podcasters' Paradise—building a prototype—John's team created a webinar and invited interested *Fire Nation* members. So instead of spending months creating content outlines and investing money up front on a course platform, John hosted a proof-of-concept webinar.

At the webinar John laid out the idea he had of creating an exclusive club for wannabe podcasters, and if enough people (fifty was the magic number) signed up for lifetime membership, John would consider his concept proven. The concept did prove out and *Fire Nation* begat Podcasters' Paradise.

Another example of an early version of a business idea: a place to crash for the night—an air mattress, workspace, Wi-

Fi, and cereal in the morning—in the apartment of Airbnb founders Joe Gebbia and Brian Chesky that they advertised to Design Conference attendees in SF.

That idea, originally dubbed AirBedandBreakfast, was developed by its founders into a business valued at ~$30B (2019)—well more than the value of the largest hotel companies anywhere. And all without the fuss and mess of owning any hotels, dealing directly with the quirks of guests, and managing an ever-evolving army of service staff.

Airbnb, as we know it, started with an email from Gebbia to Chesky in 2007 pitching an idea to make a little money on the side by renting out an air mattress in their shared apartment, complete with Wi-Fi and a desk, to young people attending a massively popular design conference in San Francisco. It would be a "designers' bed and breakfast."

The Room Where it Happened

One of my favorite examples of an early version of a production is the story of what would become the Broadway smash hit *Hamilton*. Lin-Manuel Miranda took the opportunity to perform the sixteen bars of *Hamilton* music he and his fellow performers had to work with for the President and First Lady as an invitee to the White House for Poetry Jam in 2009. Miranda had a second chance in 2012 to play a couple of numbers for Barack and Michelle Obama. The audience gave the troupe a standing O, and the reaction of the Obamas, captured on video, was exuberant.

The performance was fresh, the performers were pumped, and the crowd responded in kind. Talk about a CLICK, and a high profile one at that. Not only did Miranda put together and test an early version of his production, but he and his director, and fellow performers, created huge buzz. *Hamilton* was starting to emerge from the fertile mind of a patriot

American with Puerto Rican roots, a passion for performing rap with his drama buddies of *Freestyle Love Supreme*, and a penchant for composition, storytelling, and rhyme.

Almost any product, production, or service can first be built as an early version.

Examples of early prototypes are these:

- The manuscript in book publishing
- The alpha version in software
- The proof-of-concept prototype in medical devices
- Answer prints in moviemaking, rough cuts, test endings
- The test kitchen in the restaurant business
- A pilot episode for a new podcast, TV, or streaming series
- New craft beer recipes made in small batches for tastings
- Haute couture in fashion
- Jokes you tell your fellow comics and collaborators, or jokes you throw into your act

And here are examples of later-stage, prerelease prototypes:

- The beta version in software
- The validation and verification version in med-tech
- The galley proofs in book publishing
- Previews in movies
- A soft opening, or dry run, for a new restaurant

- Barrel tastings in the wine business
- Full sets comedians develop usually in a dingy comedy club

Amy Schumer developed her Netflix feature set doing stints at The Comedy Cellar in New York and elsewhere and reveals all the ugly details—throw-ups and all—in *Expecting Amy*, an HBO Max docuseries.

When thinking about early versions of your idea or your offering, you should use the language of your field, of course, and especially when talking to people within that field. When speaking to people outside of your field, be more descriptive in your use of language. Saying you have an early version of scenes from your movie might be easier than saying you have an answer print. An answer print is a term of art to the trade. It means nothing to lay people.

How can you be innovative with respect to prototypes? One way is to look at what people from different industries do and borrow their ideas. During the COVID-19 pandemic, people had to innovate by showing their stuff online. Can you do the same? For example, the commercial movie business uses focus groups to test movie scenes to gauge intensity and emotional level, and they test movie endings in focus groups and at test showings.

When the same comments come back repeatedly, it might be time to listen. Audience testing can reveal problems in critical areas like plot or pacing, problems that can be addressed in the editing room. Endings too can be altered as was the case famously with *Fatal Attraction* where audiences, according to the *New York Times*, "gave the thumbs way down to Glenn Close's [character] committing suicide to 'Madame Butterfly'—much preferring to see her murdered." Scenes, storylines, or characters that simply don't work for the target audience can be flagged in this manner.

And then there are real-time quantitative tracking methods that show the audience's average positive or negative reaction, relative to a neutral baseline, throughout an entire episode of entertainment.

Can you use methods like these for a creative business idea you are working on?

The National Research Group—the organization Francis Ford Coppola had a hand in creating when working on his movie *Apocalypse Now*—offers services to help the film business and others. With a little looking, you can find service providers deploying similar approaches in your field of endeavor.

How you build your prototype depends on your field, your time frame, your resources, and your constraints.

If you are in a technical field, you probably require engineering work. There may be a number of firms experienced in your area. Find out who they are and reach out to them for rough costs and lead times. There may be design or drafting studios or subcontractors you could employ. If it's a designer you seek, check online to find someone to work with. If it's a restaurant concept you want to test, see if you can find a test kitchen space to lease for a few months to test your concept.

You should be asking yourself, if you are in the early stage of developing your business idea, what the simplest working form of your product, service, or production could be. For Alli Webb it was her styling equipment, blow dryer, and her car.

Deciding whom to involve in the building of the prototype is an important consideration as well. Here are the types of perspectives/skill sets to consider:

- Designer
- Engineer
- Craftspeople

Involve them as soon as you know you want to move ahead with your creative business idea, and as soon as the basic knowledge or scientific know-how, or proof of concept, is in place. But don't stop there. Why not invite some innovative end users or influencers to the party?

Creating a prototype of your offering is a sure-fire way of figuring out if you and your team are on track. Creating an early version—something representative of the whole or something that proves your idea works—is key. With a barebones version, most businesses should test both an early version and a prerelease version. Depending on your field of endeavor, you may create many more versions than just those two.

Keep the goal in mind. Your prototype needs to CLICK with your audience.

Reflect & Act

- Figure out the typical prototypes in your field (unless you work in a scientific, medical, military, or engineering/manufacturing area, they will not likely be called prototypes). If there are no standard prototypes in your field, can you think of innovative ways of building an early or partial version of your creative business idea, possibly borrowing inspiration from other fields?

- Can you build a digital version of your product or service?

- If your prototype fails, ask yourself what this means for your idea—learn and apply to your next attempt. Adapt.

8
Blood, Sweat, and Fears

"I think this is the next nail salon. I think this is going to kill it. Let's do it," Alli Webb told her husband.

As we learned in the last chapter, Webb discovered a gap in the women's hairstyling space that she and her partners filled by creating a bricks-and-mortar blowout salon, Drybar.

Webb's mobile blowout dry run worked out extremely well—there was demand for her service—and Webb piqued the interest of both her husband, Cameron, an art director at an ad agency, and her brother, Michael, a financially savvy guy ex of Yahoo, with the idea of creating a bricks-and-mortar salon that would focus on blowout hairstyling.

The trio enlisted an architect, Josh, who became part of the team that would create this archetype.

Together, the four of them designed the look and feel and the functionality for the salon. Webb knew what kind of experience she wanted to create for her guests and what the stylists would need to feel energized and to be able to do their best work.

"I knew I wanted it to feel like a bar."

Her husband had the flair for branding and color elements, which he brought into the physical space and to the website. Her brother was thinking about the business aspects and maybe even the replicability of this first release bricks-and-mortar salon.

Webb said designing and building the first salon was a lot of fun, during an interview with Guy Raz: "We had the perfect skill sets, we were like this powerhouse, nobody had to pay us."

The first audience you have to impress is yourself.

It's a satisfying feeling to create something that is an expression of yourself and your collaborators. The alchemy of a small group of people designing and building together can be a powerful force.

As the creator of a product, service, or creative production, you know when you have done your best work. If you're proud of your design, you have met the test of one essential audience, the creators.

"I'm just going to do it the way I want to do it, not the way it's always been done," said Webb.

Having enthused customers with the styling results Webb and her curated team of stylists could deliver and design and having built a salon with the feel of a bar and the function of a salon, Drybar was well on its way. Having Webb's brother and husband as part of the creative team meant that the initial source of investment—bootstrapping—was on board.

There was one important group left to captivate: the influencers. The first ones to help spread enthusiasm for Drybar were the writers from the *Daily Candy* publication who wrote a story when Drybar was about to open its doors for the first time.

Drybar opened in style.

Customers First

You've assembled your team, shaped your creative business idea, and started to build your offering. I encourage you to start testing versions of your product, service, or production early and often. At a minimum you should test until you have a version that works and your prerelease version.

Test the early version to prove your concept, to see how well your product works and learn how to improve it. Test the prerelease prototype to gauge how customers and key people react to its near-ready design garb. This can help you to tweak your offering and build anticipation for your full release version.

As with many approaches in this book, there are two types of audiences to test and refine your beta version with: internal audiences and external audiences.

I use CLICK as an acronym to cover the people you will want to test your offering with, or the people you will want to share your results with—at least the positive results.

C-L-I-C-K

C = Customers
L = Lab (Technical) People
I = Investors
C = Creators
K = Key Opinion Leaders

THE FIVE ESSENTIAL AUDIENCES: CUSTOMERS, LAB/TECH PEOPLE, INVESTORS, CREATORS, AND KEY OPINION LEADERS

Not all of these audiences need to see all of your versions, nor do they need to see them in the same way. So, first, customers.

Customers

A very simple testing approach is to take a working version of your creative business idea to meetups or conferences where your intended users go, set up a simple testing table or area, and invite people to pass through and sample your early version. Prepare for this revealing with any questions you may want answered. It can be a great way to sit with future customers and hear from them directly.

The director of iGate, the incubator in California where I worked as a mentor and start-up community builder, held an evening devoted to user testing for its member companies and members. I took the opportunity to test a user interface my team had been working on for an online surveying tool. I remember it being an exciting experience. The event was a blast for start-up team members and testers alike.

Performing pilot tests and creating early access to your offering can be useful learning and promotional experiences for you.

As chronicled in the *Edmonton Sun*, Sameer Dhar, along with cofounders Tim Ahong and Jeremy Dabor of Sensassure, spent a ton of time identifying a worthwhile, solvable problem—the burden to senior care professionals and inconvenience to incontinent nursing home residents of adult diaper changing.

Once the trio determined that innovation in the form of a sensor might solve the problem of untimely diaper changing, the team took a rapid prototyping approach directly to their intended customers, testing, iterating, and testing again different sensor designs. At one point the team lived and worked among two nursing homes in Maryland so they could test their prototypes with diaper-dependent residents and talk with the nurses responsible for keeping those diapers fresh.

The company's final product was so impressive they sold their company to the global hygiene company Essity AB for around $5M—a strong return on the young founders' efforts. Time lapse from the initial SPARK to the GO of a sale was less than two years.

Lab (Technical) People

Your offering must prove to be reliable and valid. It must do what you claim it will do. The tests you create to prove your claims will vary depending on the domain in which your business operates. In some fields there may not be an objective measure of performance.

Your "lab" may be a series of servers. It could be an animation, voice or video editing studio, a test kitchen, a performance room, the street, an arena, a fitness studio, or an actual scientific, medical, or engineering lab with powers to grant you, or not grant you, a license.

For Lin-Manuel Miranda, one of his labs was a makeshift performance space in the bottom of the Drama Book Shop in midtown Manhattan where he performed as part of the improvisational rap ensemble *Freestyle Love Supreme*.

Labs might give some kind of a seal of approval that you can then leverage.

Investors

Investors will be mainly interested in how your prototype testing is establishing the feasibility and likely performance of your offering with customers.

Of course, you should feel free to give them a demo—the sharks on *Shark Tank* always seem to love this. They love it even more if your business is aiming at the unmet needs of lots of customers.

Investors may be close to you and your boat, or they may be attached to accelerators that you may be working with. You can even sometimes find them as judges for start-up pitches like the ones at Startup Weekend and similar start-up group sponsors. Awards make for terrific validation and fodder for promotion.

But if you and your cofounders in the business are the only investors—you are bootstrapping, for example, or have put in some seed capital—then you should pause, put on your investor hat, and take a look at your solution and business opportunity from an investment point of view. You want to ask yourself if your sweat equity and other resources going into your business are likely to yield an acceptable return.

Creators

You and your team, if you have one, are the first people to judge whether what you are creating is the jam. You know if you are producing a quality product or not, and over time you will become an even better judge.

Julia Louis-Dreyfus told Seth Meyers during a *Seinfeld* reunion fund-raiser in October of 2020 that she and her fellow cast members, along with Larry David, Jerry Seinfeld, and the director, knew during table reads and rehearsals if they had something worthy of their own show, as they were creating it.

So fire up that inner critic and make sure you meet your own tough standards.

Key Opinion Leaders

Key opinion leaders (KOLs) are the experts, the bloggers, the social media mavens with a zillion Instagram and TikTok fans, the media folks—writers and broad or narrow casters covering your space—the critics, and even the celebrities big and small. KOLs can add street cred to your cause and credibility to your venture in the eyes of investors and others. Identifying influencers and CLICKing with some of them early in the development of your creative business idea creates momentum.

So those are the main audiences with whom you want your offering to CLICK: customers, lab/technical people, investors, creators (yourself), and key opinion leaders (influencers).

Regardless of the group judging your product, you are testing two main factors with your prototype:

1. Feasibility: Does it work?

2. Performance: To what degree does it work?

And typically hurdles such as these, depending on which group you are appealing to, include

- Ease of use
- Reliability
- Safety
- Operating cost
- Emotional reaction

If your idea works, you have a proof of concept. There's hope. If it doesn't work, start again.

As soon as you have proof that your solution works, you and your team will be asked these questions:

- How well does it work?
- How efficient is it?
- How does it compare to thing-a-ma-bob x?
- Is it easy to use and safe?
- Are there impacts on the environment?

And people will want to try it, which could be fantastic—or not—so be ready.

Prototype Testing: Key Questions for the Five Essential Audiences

Customers

- Does your solution meet a critical need of your intended customers?
- Is your solution strongly attractive to your intended customers at a price point likely to be profitable?
- Are customers saying they will buy your product/service with a frequency appropriate for your goals to be met?
- How excited are your intended customers about your offering?

Lab (Technical) People

- Does your offering work according to your goals and claims?
- Do you have empirical proof?

- Can you reliably produce the offering you tested to a high quality standard?
- Are there any safety or environmental issues with your product?
- If you had collaborators, judges, or an audience involved, was the emotional reaction positive?

Investors

- Does your product, the market you are aiming to create or pursue, and the business model you are proposing interest and excite investors?
- Do your performance results meet the hurdle your investors think is needed?
- Can you see your investors coming on board to fund your endeavor?

Creators

- Are you and the people involved in creating your offering pleased with the direction your creative business idea is going?
- Does the version of your offering you are testing work, and does it perform to the level you expected—to the level you need to score a win?
- Are you super proud of your prerelease version?

Key Opinion Leaders

- Do the influencers in your field like what they see in your product or service or production?

- Do experts in your field recognize the value of your solution?

- Do bloggers and media have a favorable view of your solution, and are they attracted to you and your team and what you bring to the field?

- Do you see potential for any of these opinion leaders becoming ambassadors for your business?

Before I worked in start-ups and with early-stage companies, I worked in the pharmaceutical business. Here we had what we called target product profiles (TPPs). The target profile made clear what we wanted a new product to do, and not do. The basic pattern: compelling clinical benefits with minimal side effects.

While we could not take the actual drug out to doctors to use, except through our clinical research people in controlled settings, we could and did take the target product profiles out to potential users to gauge their reactions.

We used either one-on-one interviews or group sessions. We typically had an objective third party carry out customer research for us. That helped us meet our goal, which was always to get realistic and objective reactions to what we were creating.

Our third-party researcher prepared a list of questions she would ask the potential user to understand situations where the product might be used and how often, whether the product might take the place of another one currently available or be used in combination with other measures.

Meanwhile, our research and development folks had tests to measure the performance of a new molecule in areas like blood concentration levels, impact on biomarkers such as cholesterol levels, and changes in functional variables like heart rate. Clinical trials were conducted to see if a drug was safe and could improve health outcomes.

In short, a new product had to meet or exceed objective measures and standards of performance. When positive objective measures and results from controlled tests are combined with learnings from customer research, your direction and progress can take off.

What might you have that would be relevant in your domain? Can you measure speed, or capacity, or money saved by using your product, for example?

Not all products, services, or productions need this type of rigorous testing, of course. In some cases, the main measure to go on is the emotional reaction of your audience or users.

When I lived in California, I spent time working on a company whose principal product was software users subscribed to, which was designed to help customers intelligently price their offerings using a variety of relevant external data. It was a brilliant idea.

For the company's product, as with any product, a key test was whether the software worked. Could the software do what we claimed? Could it increase earnings by up to 40 percent among the clients who deployed it?

On one level the software worked well. We could link a user's account to their platform account; we could comb the data and get a feel for demand; we could apply our algorithm to the numbers and post new prices to our clients' orders on the platform.

But did it work?

Our users wanted to see more demand. That was their key measurement. Did we build something to do that? We're not sure. We were claiming that they could make more money by using our software compared to not using our software and that was, of course, after the 1 percent commission charge. But we couldn't definitively prove an increase in demand.

And our users could not prove it themselves. They were trapped in the single universe scenario. The lack of a control group blocked them from ever knowing. They could not tell if, or to what degree, it was working.

One thing we did know. We were experiencing churn, loss of accounts, at a faster rate than desired. That told us that some of our clients were not seeing enough value to remain loyal. The lack of a clear test that the solution worked was a major problem.

Digital-first ad testing is becoming advocated as a way in which advertisers can test their products—their ads—before running with them to wider distribution.

According to Britt Nolan of Leo Burnett, "[Quantitative surveys] are great for preventing disasters. But if you are trying to learn what real people in the real world want to seek out and engage with, quant isn't going to help you."

Nolan suggests YouTube is a better focus group than using quantitative surveys to see what people click on and watch. Running ads on YouTube first allows for a quick gut level check and "optimization on the fly."

That's the kind of testing with users and product adjustment you want to make when you are operating in the real world but have not yet fully launched.

Apple used a prototype of its next generation Macs—the first to use Apple-designed chips—at its June 2020 Developer Conference to demonstrate how apps designed for iPhones and iPads would run, for the first time, unchanged on the new Macs. Your MacBook is going to look like a clam-shaped iPhone. No doubt before this demo, they tested this internally in myriad ways.

As *Wired* magazine observed about a game, a guitar tutorial, and a meditation app demo, "When running on one of the upcoming Apple Silicon Macs, all of those, to use a term Apple loves, *simply worked*."

In this way a test of a prerelease version becomes a massive publicity stunt.

During the COVID-19 crisis, as I am writing this, I am working as part of a team developing a direct protein detection method for possible deployment at scale to detect and monitor SARS-CoV-2, the novel coronavirus that causes

COVID-19. I became the team's de facto field representative watching what the FDA was doing to allow more test developers like us to develop and deploy our technology.

Medical device testing can be quite specific and rigorous. During the pandemic, and to the FDA's credit, the agency gave specific advice on exactly what kinds of tests should be done in order to receive emergency use authorization. This guidance and their reporting requirements made it possible for more tests to hit the market sooner than if they had made no changes to their testing and filing protocols.

The agency also allowed a lot of creative leeway for developers seeking to prove something specific for their devices, especially in areas of highest need with the least amount of collective experience.

You may or may not have specific guidance, and you may not need something so rigorous, but most companies can benefit by objective proof-points about their products and services, and especially when joined with user feedback.

Reflect & Act

- It's vital that the early and prerelease versions of your offering be tested with internal and external audiences to see if they CLICK. Your early version is your first working version. Your prerelease version is near final form.

- Design internal tests now to make sure your product, service, or production works and to what degree. Adapt and improve as necessary.

- Test your offering primarily with customers but include investors, lab/technical people, collaborators, and key opinion leaders as appropriate to the field you are operating in.

9
Promises, Promises

To love and to hold you ...

Don't worry, I won't let go.

Pizza to your doorstep in 30 minutes or less—or it's free.

The check's in the mail.

I'll call you.

Branding starts as a promise that you attach to your chosen name and logo, but it does not end there; that is only the beginning.

Google was a name that meant nothing until people started using it to search the internet. Now it has reached verb status. It has become something that means *to search*—and so much more.

Google became a name that meant something and a service we could all trust because they delivered on the basic search promise. We typed in a search term and, presto, out came results, thousands of them in a split second—the most relevant links at the top of the list.

Now when the company brings out a new product, they start at a place of trust, at least with me, because I use their products all day, every day to search, communicate, and document. I would not have written this book without Google at my fingertips.

Just as trust is built every time a Google search result comes back with something useful—and I will always love Google for that—trust can be eroded.

Google—in this case, NEST home security devices, a Google company—was taken to task in early 2019 for not informing customers that their nifty thermostats contained microphones. Once the intrusion on privacy was discovered, Google admitted the microphones were in the devices, but said they had not been activated in the homes of millions. They said they were sorry for not informing their loyal legion of fans. Sorry, Google—you lost me on that one.

Either the response was completely disingenuous, and the company was simply denying something because it made them look, dare I say, evil, or they were completely insensitive to customers' privacy concerns when they chose not to inform customers that their NEST thermostats contained microphones.

I was shocked many years prior when Google started delivering advertising via Gmail—but I stuck with the service. I guess this is a sign that I really trusted the company, and I do. Google Drive, the most intuitive cloud storage I have used—and I have used a lot of them—contains more about my life than I know. Google Chrome knows more about my surfing history than I do. Google search knows all the questions I've asked it in the past decades. Holy cow, Batman.

Google promises great design in products that work and can be counted on. They promise to make my life—and yours—better and easier. That's a brand promise I will stick with as long as they live up to it every day, which is exactly what you need to do with your brand.

Brand names, logos, tag lines, colors, fonts, style palettes—all of these need to resonate with your intended customers.

They should SPARK an immediate feeling of, "Ah yes, that looks like a brand or a solution for x." Do your logos, the look and feel of your physical establishment or online property, or advertisements you have created CLICK with intended customers? If not, keep working.

Likable Logos

In September of 2019, Micah Lally of Bluleadz, a digital sales and marketing design agency, posted a roundup of the "30 Most Recognizable Brand Logos of All Time" to the agency's blog, an ambitious project.

Among the logos making the list were these:

- Nike
- Disney
- Microsoft
- Starbucks
- Lacoste's cute alligator

Lally: "Your logo is the symbol attached to your brand that's meant to help identify it. A logo communicates to the world what it is you offer, what your values are, and what sets you apart from other businesses in your industry."

Superb packaging stands out from the crowd, does the containment and protection job efficiently, reflects the brand, and positions the product at a desired tier in the market.

The Right Package

Dan Aykroyd, aka Elwood Blues, as in the Blues Brothers, as in, "We're on a mission from God," is an actor, comedian, and entrepreneur. He's known for his work on *SNL* and my favorite skit of his: The Super Bass-O-Matic '76 (YouTube it), *Ghostbusters*, *Trading Places*, *Driving Miss Daisy*, and for *The Blues Brothers* movie. He's a musician, a fellow Canuck, and an accomplished entrepreneur having cofounded the House of Blues in 1992.

In 2005, Aykroyd started a company to import Patrón tequila into Canada through which he created his own original brand, Crystal Head Vodka—an award-winning pure spirit—with partner and artist John Alexander. Crafted by Globefill Inc., the white spirit is derived from pure water from Newfoundland and a particular type of corn (instead of potatoes or grains) called Peaches and Cream from southwestern Ontario. (I can tell you P&C corn is delicious, as is a similar maize you can find in New Jersey under the name bi-color corn—talk about lousy branding.)

In a BBC article, Aykroyd is quoted as saying "that the bottle design was chosen as a nod to the legend that ancient tribes across the Americas used crystal skulls in religious ceremonies." And that "the vodka has now sold more than 13 million bottles." The bottle design is a work of art, finely molded by the Italian company Bruni Glass (Milan), bringing flair and pedigree to the bottle.

Crystal Head's tag line, "Nothing but Pure Spirit," connects us to the mystery of the spiritual realm and speaks to the purity of the liquid—no glycerols, citrus oils, or sugars added. The packaging is a perfect reflection of the brand name and works in harmony to create the mystique of the brand just as flawlessly as the semiprecious stones, known as Herkimer diamonds, do—the ones that filter the spirit during the distilling process.

The brand has won awards for distinctiveness—Wikipedia listed eleven awards from the US and Australia, and one for taste from the home of vodka, Russia.

Crystal Head's offerings are priced in the upper echelon of vodkas. Per my findings of a search of the online offerings from retailer Total Wine, Crystal Head Vodka starts at $49 a bottle and rises from there with special editions, placing the brand above nearly four hundred offerings on the site.

Clearly, packaging can help aim a brand at a desired tier of customers. Crystal Head Vodka is an ultra-premium brand that comes in finely crafted bottles designed by its artistic cofounder. Its ingredients, celebrity, origin story, and the brand's very presence are distilled into pure spirit.

Another spirit worth sampling: Johnny Walker. Johnny Walker is coming out with a paper bottle for its Black Label whiskey. Yes, paper. The bottle will be black with a matte finish and white lettering according to *Fast Company* (July 2020). The label promises to reduce the environmental footprint for its products and positions the business as forward-thinking. The packaging innovation will give connoisseurs, marketers, and enviro-driven folks something to talk about over a dram or two.

Shall we stay on the theme of packaging? My wife and I live in an apartment in the historic Charlestown neighborhood of Boston. The brick building, built in 1850, was once a manor house. In 1920, a wing was added. If the building was a letter, it would be a capital L. My wife works at the foot of the L, and I work near its head. We meet in the middle when we are not working.

When I peer up from my desk, I see a glorious park. We are immersed in monuments commemorating battles from the War of Independence—I can picture American revolutionaries valiantly fighting British redcoats right here at Breed's Hill.

While this is an inspiring place to live and work, and the L shape is wonderful for livability, the Wi-Fi is not stellar. After numerous tries, my neighbor told me he was using eero to extend his Wi-Fi network. Eero is a fantastic product that has created one giant Wi-Fi happiness zone for us where once there were dead zones.

I bring up eero because its packaging reflects a strong brand promise. Eero is and looks expensive, and the packaging reflects a strong brand promise—one the company must deliver on time and again.

The eero box with lots of blank white space and crisp red graphics is an homage to Steve Jobs and Jony Ive. The box is the size and shape of a Trivial Pursuit board game and is constructed to the same quality. The cardboard has a nice satiny feel to it. I hated to throw it out.

The brand promise was made clear by its outer look: "This stuff is well-designed and worth every penny—it will bring you Wi-Fi wherever you need it," said the box. And it has.

My only knock on eero is the recyclability of the packaging. It has foam glued to the bottom of the box that cannot easily be removed, making it a reject for our blue recycle bin. Maybe eero wants me to keep the box forever, like a board game? Not sure.

Similar to the Mac and iPhone and anything from Apple, the package is beautiful—it is designed to look like it carries something of exquisite design, and it does, right down to the minimalist instruction leaflet. These businesses have thought this through to the delight of their customers. Pay attention to products and services you encounter for the first time and what the packaging *says* to you. There's going to be a test.

One of the worst moves you can make is to price and package your offering expensively and then not deliver. To do so is to exploit what is known in the trade as price illusion—the idea that people associate higher priced goods with higher quality.

Your packaging should absolutely reflect your values and the values of your customers.

Think about your effect on the environment and what your choices say about you when you develop your packaging, because, duh, there is just one environment. Nothing bugs me more—okay, cancer does—than organic vegetables packed in massive amounts of plastic. I don't get it. If a supplier is going to be earth friendly, they should be earth friendly 360 degrees. Do the people who select organic food only focus on what the food might do for their bodies and not care about the environment? I doubt it.

Subaru has zero emission plants—how the hell is that possible? Kudos to them.

On Messaging

Who wins the prize for consistency in messaging? Here are some famous messages that have withstood the test of time:

- "You're in good hands with x."
- "Good to the last drop."
- "Have it your way at x."
- The x: "All the news that's fit to print."

Do you know who these companies are? How many can you identify?

> "You're in good hands with *Allstate*."
> "Good to the last drop." *Maxwell House* coffee
> "Have it your way at Burger King."
> The *New York Times*: "All the news that's fit to print."

The tag lines or slogans for the businesses in this list have not changed much over time because they speak to the brands' promise. Allstate insurance will take care of you. Maxwell House is always great coffee, even when you get to the dregs. The royal servants at Burger King will make you a burger the way you want it—hold the raw onions, please.

The *New York Times* promises to be comprehensive but does not do yellow journalism.

How will you get your message across? Don't be pedantic. Be clever.

Here's an idea I had for messaging to patients about a cholesterol-reducing medicine that my team and I were responsible for in Canada: "CRESTOR: works with or without willpower." It's better, don't you think, than this message: "Whether you restrict saturated fats and cholesterol in your diet or not, CRESTOR will help you." We never used it, but it was the kind of tongue-in-cheek message that might work with patients.

The sign at Bob's, a grocery, beer, and wine store in the Italian area of the North End of Boston, says *convenience* in a creative way: "If we don't have it, you don't need it."

Here's another clever way to make a case. You could shout from the rooftops about the quality of your coffee beans, or you could say something like, "Handpicked by Juan Valdez." This was the tag line that helped put Columbian coffee into the minds, and cups, of many.

"We're number two, so we try harder." So claimed Avis, then the rival to the leading rental car agency in the US, Hertz. According to Jim Edwards, of *Business Insider* in August 2012, the "we try harder" tag line was penned by Paula Green in 1962 after the then-number-two car rental company tried to explain to its new ad agency, DDB, why anyone would choose the runner-up brand over Hertz, the biggest company.

It's the kind of message that takes a humbling fact about a company, being smaller in this case, and turns it into an appealing strength. Who wouldn't want clean ashtrays, heaters that heat, and a pleasant smile when they pick up their rental car?

Tell Your Story

To be a creative business idea, your idea, your business must be a unique reflection of you. This means the idea reflects your passions, your interests, and your values. Therefore, messaging about your business is effective if it draws people into your passions, interests, and values.

Everything you do from branding to messaging to design and delivery of your product or service is a reflection of you. Customers who identify with who you are as a business and as a person will be loyal customers who will attract people in their network to your business.

Today a lot of communication is two-way with avenues such as Twitter and Instagram open to customers and to companies. This means the people doing the communicating for you need to be a true reflection of your values—they need to treat customers the way you would.

People want to get to know and do business with companies with whom their values align, and they want to know your story. Fantastic. That is a perfect fit with the kind of business I'm encouraging you to create—one that is a true reflection of you and your cofounders.

Craft a CRISP Message

I learned about messaging as part of the MBA I earned in London. Well, at Canada's well-respected business school, the Ivey School of Business in London, Ontario. At the time, businesses communicated about their products and services with customers in a one-sided way.

The dominant forms of communication were advertisements for which market researchers and agency communication people crafted and tested ads for features like stopping power and the potential to change the customer's behavior in some way.

Here's a powerful way to direct your messaging.

Philippe Latapie heads up the consulting agency StratX (now StratX ExL) that I have been affiliated with since moving to the US in the early 2000s. Phil has been a friend of mine since I went to work for him first as a business development guy and later as a consultant/facilitator. He and I created the following mnemonic to capture what we thought was important for positioning a product via messaging:

CRISP

- Clear and compelling
- Relevant
- Inspiring
- Sustainable
- Provable

The idea is to use this rubric to craft your main message—the message that meshes with the core need of your intended audience—and that serves as a theme around which various submessages or campaigns are built.

The mantra of SPARK-CLICK-GO is testing. Bringing a creative business idea to life usually requires lots of testing, but sometimes it goes fast and sometimes you make it up as you go along like that cartoon character walking off the edge of a building seemingly into midair if it were not for steel girders placed beneath his feet in succession just in time.

Sometimes elements of the journey come fast like the original idea, and sometimes a new product goes all the way from idea to reality fast.

An example of something moving from SPARK to CLICK to GO swiftly (in five days) is the song "Satisfaction," as in, "I can't get no," which, according to *Rolling Stone* magazine, came to Keith Richards almost complete in a dream like manna from heaven one night in 1965 while the band was not well known.

At the time the Stones were midway through their third US tour, their only bona fide American hits to date were "Time Is on My Side" and the then recently released "The Last Time." They recorded the song a few days later in Chicago and finished it two days after that in a Hollywood studio.

So in five days that song, one of the defining songs of the Rolling Stones to this day, was conceived, shaped, and recorded in its final form. "Satisfaction" catapulted the Rolling Stones into rock superstardom.

Forty years later, *Rolling Stone* put the following historical perspective on the riff Keith Richards discovered that day in May 1965: "That spark in the night … was the crossroads: the point at which the rickety jump and puppy love of early rock and roll became rock."

Richards would say on a *Sunday Morning* CBS interview with Anthony Mason in 2016 that "the song gets more interesting" the more he plays it, and that after more than fifty years he's "starting to get the hang of it"—finding little licks here and there that he wished he'd have put on the record.

The song was ranked second only to Bob Dylan's "Like a Rolling Stone" on *Rolling Stone* magazine's self-proclaimed definitive list of the greatest rock songs of all time, published in April 2011.

Thinking Fast and Slow

The initial impetus for "Satisfaction" came quickly and so did the writing of the song. In many cases, the original idea—the SPARK—comes quickly, but the CLICK and GO bits, the development, the testing, the releasing—takes years.

The idea for the musical *Hamilton*—the SPARK—as Lin-Manuel Miranda relayed on an interview on the Disney streaming channel in July of 2020 came to him before he had finished reading the second chapter of *Alexander Hamilton* by Ron Chernow, while on a beach vacation. But the execution of the idea—all the writing and recording and casting and arranging—took many years.

Test the Softer Elements of Your Offering

"Branding, packaging, and message testing you must," Yoda says.

I've done very professional branding, messaging, and advertising research, which is kinda the most fun, as well as packaging testing and a revamp of labels. Depending on the size of your business, and what's at stake, you may want to spend some big bucks to get these soft elements of your business right.

For example, if you are signing off on packaging artwork that will then be used by hundreds of thousands of users, and for which you will be billed even bigger bucks to make changes to, it might be worth the money to professionally test your creations.

When I was with Knoll Pharmaceuticals, we underwent a packaging change that basically used a much bigger font for the dosage and changed the layout to make a key number stand out. There was no need to test this.

In the med-tech space, getting the packaging down and the instructions for use correct is essential for patients to understand how to use our products.

User testing—also known as human factors testing and its design counterpart cleverly called human factors design—is essential to see if real people can understand how to use your product or service.

At StratX, the boutique consultancy I work with, we call this ethnographic research. Picture Jane Goodall among her chimps in what is now the Gombe National Forest, Tanzania, and you know what is meant by ethnographic research. The idea being to fade into the background of the subject's habitat so you can observe the behaviors of interest.

A/B testing, for example, is a process for determining which of two offerings or advertisements is more effective.

When I worked with a software-as-a-service company in California, we would develop two versions of an ad and let both run on Facebook, then take a look at the data to see which resulted in better click-throughs to our website, and to better conversion. This is standard web traffic monitoring. You can do the same with most things on the web.

Even more valuable would be to think about A/B testing as a mindset. Once you've developed something that works, whether in the physical or virtual world, keep going unless you can beat it with an alternative. If you can replace an aging version (A) with something your customers like more (B), maybe you should do so.

Packaging testing is probably best done physically—at least your subjects should be with the packages you are working with—but the visuals, just like with branding and messaging artwork and text, can be easily tested online. It doesn't have to be onerous. As the shoe god says—Just Do It.

A brand is a promise. It's as simple as that. A creative business idea is, by definition, a reflection of you in some way. That means you are promising something to your customers, and they will hold you to it.

The packaging you choose for your offering is the first impression new customers will come across. It should be attractive, functional, and in keeping with your values. It should be a beacon for your brand. What you say about your business, how you say it, and how your employees embody the message of your business is essential to attracting people to your business. Tell your story. Talk up the value you provide. Be the brand.

Reflect & Act

- Think about the promise inherent in your business offering and how you can attract people to, and deliver on, that promise.

- What does your creative business idea look like as a brand? How would it be packaged?

- How can you best tell the story of how you came into being and why? Can you ensure your messaging is CRISP? What is the best way to talk about the value customers should expect to derive from becoming a customer?

10
Perpetual Money-Making Machine

On a golden day in May 2012, the week of the Facebook IPO, incidentally, I visited Stanford University in Palo Alto, California, about an hour's drive from Livermore. The campus is unlike the campuses of my youth. A palm-tree–lined boulevard leads up to Memorial Court, which serves as a welcoming area within the main quad. The buildings' arches and red-clay roofs, reminiscent of the Spanish missions that dot the California coast, were exotic to my Canadian sensibilities.

In the more modern Huang Engineering Center, another installment of the Entrepreneurial Thought Leader lecture series was about to start. It's an event open to the public (in person and online) but is mainly attended by eager computer science and engineering students. The guest entrepreneur I came to see was Daniel Ek, the founder of Spotify, the online platform for music (and now podcast) discovery, sharing, and playback.

At the time, I was thrilled to have Pandora for my go-to music app. I loved creating stations, playlists generated by Pandora based on the DNA of the song or artist selected, and the whole business built on the backbone of the Music Genome Project—a genius idea.

As much as I loved then, and still love, Pandora, what Daniel Ek was offering sounded even better—the ability for a Spotify user to access any song at any time and create and share what they were discovering or playing with friends and others in the community online, all for a low monthly fee.

Since I had never grabbed onto Apple's iTunes service—buying songs piecemeal for 99 cents—I was therefore *not* chained to a collection of digital songs. Spotify sounded perfect to me. And my street cred went up a peck or two with my teenage kids since I had the scoop on what would become a streaming phenomenon.

Speaking at the forum in Stanford was not a way to gain new Spotify customers for Ek. His flight costs—to cover nine time zones and thousands of miles from Sweden to California—and travel expenses would measure in thousands against new revenues in the hundreds. It wouldn't be sustainable, and it wouldn't be a scalable customer acquisition approach.

Spotify didn't need Ek to stump for his own brand in person—his online music app was growing its users by about 50 percent at the time. So what was the customer acquisition approach Spotify was deploying that was part of the growth in users the business was enjoying? Integration with Facebook.

Ek relayed the story of how he, Mark Zuckerberg, and Sean Parker (of Napster infamy) concluded that making Spotify-sourced music widely available, and shareable via Facebook's user feeds, would create a fantastic user experience leveraging music as social object.

"Music transcends culture and geographies, and communicates an emotion," said Ek.

Spotify had worked hard to unlock the music vaults of companies like Universal music through licensing deals, promising them better returns than their current cut from iTunes at 99 cents per song and help with their pirating problem. Now Spotify had the world's biggest platform through which to disseminate awareness of that access. Brilliant.

Ek did not make clear during the Entrepreneurial Thought Leader forum that day in May of 2012 what the fiduciary deal was between Spotify and Facebook, but this observer bets his cost per new user attracted via FB is on the order of single dollars, against yearly revenues on the order of hundreds.

Having a cost of getting a new customer dramatically lower than your revenues from the customer is a key component of a business model that CLICKs.

Daniel Ek's story of marrying easy-to-access music on demand from a desperate music industry to a social network with the desire to connect the world's inhabitants is inspiring. Ek wanted to make all the world's music available to anybody with an internet connection, anywhere, anytime. That was the itch he was scratching for himself and for others. He and his team built a digital service that was a winning alternative to piracy.

His offering beat iTunes and Pandora too. Ek and team found a way for its users to access all the world's songs (okay, not all) without having to buy them or wait for the desired song to be played by an algorithm. He deployed original and imaginative ideas by cracking the licensing nut and giving users a simple dashboard to the digital vaults.

Spotify is a creative business idea that just works because it's easy for users to play, discover, and share music from any device. It's an attractive story and a compelling offering.

So, too, is your story. The story at the heart of your creative business idea. That story is a magnet that will pull people toward your creative business idea. A second magnet is your deployment of imaginative or original ideas.

What will keep people in your orbit will be the value they derive from your offering. So tell people your story, how it is that you, uniquely, came up with your business idea. Tell them about your view of the world, about the problem you are working to solve, the need you are fulfilling.

The more people understand your use of imaginative or original ideas to meet a need they have, the more those people will gravitate in your direction. How can they resist?

Here are two simple truths about customer acquisition:

1. You need a method that works.

2. That method needs to cost less per customer than the return you earn.

Let's break down the math.

A method that works means that you have experimented with approaches and settled on one that it is efficient and repeatable. A method that works finds prospects that fit your target description, or are interested in your offering, and converts them (like one kind of electricity into another, or euros into pesos), from prospects into customers.

Woodworking furniture maker Dallas Gara could pay for Google AdWords, for example, that target people searching for

- Handmade wood furniture for sale, and,

- Who live within a reasonable radius of his wood shop.

As long as the bid Gara pays to acquire one paying customer is a lot lower than the profit he makes per furniture item sold, he's happy.

He's happy unless or until there is a different method of acquiring customers that is more efficient or more reliable. Hint: The best practice is to find one solid method of customer acquisition—call it plan A—and then see if you can find a second method, which you then add to your repertoire like arrows to a quiver, or to replace plan A.

Another method Gara could employ would be constantly priming social media where he has more than 10,000 followers. That is a beautiful start, especially if his followers are within his serviceable shipping area (the world—at the right price), or he could blog about the craft of woodworking.

Folks, there are two ways to acquire customers: you go to them, or they come to you.

Consider these customer acquisition methods:

- Word of mouth
- Augmented word of mouth (this means paid spots that accelerate or more widely distribute spots in which your customers praise and recommend you)
- Social media advertising
- Blogging
- Advertising
- Search engine optimization (SEO)
- Outbound sales
- Inbound sales
- Tapping into someone else's customers (such as via distributors)
- Sales force
- Partnering/bundling
- PR
- Events
- Algorithmic recommendation (cool stuff here—Netflix is the king of this)

Your job is to figure out one customer acquisition method that works well. Use trial and error to get you there.

Experiment. Try out a few techniques in advance of your first release. Measure your results and your costs.

When I was with a software company in California, we figured out that online targeted ads worked well as a way of finding new clients at a low cost compared to expected revenues.

Get a customer acquisition method going and then add to it if you need more. For Daniel Ek, Facebook was the first big customer acquisition method he and his team went after. It worked.

You Are Not the Kardashians

In almost any line of work, if you have an audience, you can translate that to a business you love. If you have a ton of followers on social media, that is the first place to go if you have a new business you are creating or launching.

Witness the Kardashians. Or Mark Cuban. Steve Case. Guy Kawasaki. Barbara Corcoran. Tim Ferriss.

It's probably helpful if the reason you are attracting and engaging your followers is related to your creative business idea. If you comment a lot on people's fashions or post a lot of yourself being fashionable, that can probably be translated into a fashion business.

If your posts are all about fishing, you probably won't translate your followers into fashion customers—unless the fashion is fishing. That could be a thing—handsome waders and iridescent camo toques for ice fishing—you get the drift (*toque* BTW is Canadian for wool hat—it's pronounced like fluke with a T, don't ask, the French started it).

If you don't have a lot of social media followers in an area related to your business idea, can you start something in the early phases to create a following? For example, if you're thinking about a premium pet toy or food business, ask Fluffy if you can set up an Instagram account for her and start snapping away.

Your creative business idea is digital, isn't it? What I mean is that virtually any business idea you are thinking of creating is either full-on digital or it has a digital component, no?

Dallas Gara spends his time creating handmade wood furniture based on craftsmanship he has been developing throughout his life. When it comes to promoting and selling his one-of-a-kinds, he does so online.

Every business has a digital component, and every buyer (well, maybe not every buyer, but damn near every buyer) at least searches, reads reviews, or buys online.

According to Statista (referenced online by Bankmycell), there are 3.5 billion smartphones in the world today. In the ten most advanced countries, roughly three out of four people have a smartphone. That's a lot of search capability that could be put to work looking for your business.

Blogging will help interested parties find you. Why? Because the search gremlins know how to find you. They call it SEO—search engine optimization. It can really help your business. Google it.

Love the One You're With

The best way to retain customers is to provide them value.
    The best way to retain customers is to provide them value.
    Oops, I repeated that sentence.
    The best way to retain customers is to provide them value.
    There it is again. I must really mean it.
    The second-best way is to create a bond with them.
    The third best way is to create a habit.
    The fourth best way is to make it difficult or costly for them to switch.

This applies of course to business where repeat use is important, which probably applies to most businesses. For nuclear power plants you may only sell one to a given customer, though that is hardly a reason to argue against the creation of compelling value.

The more your customers identify with your story and with the values projected by the culture of your creative business idea, the more likely they will be to stick with you. It will be natural.

Let's look at each of these methods:

1. Create value.

2. Create a bond.

3. Create a habit.

4. Create lock-in.

Create Value

First, provide customers with value. If your creative business idea is unique and you are the first one in a space, think about creating value so strong that new entrants will have a difficult time attracting your customers away.

Always be adding value (ABAV). In fact, make yourself obsolete; make your second version bring more value than the first; make the experience better, more rewarding, special in some way for repeat users or premium payers; add features; lower costs (direct and indirect); raise performance levels like Toyota does by bringing safety technology to all the cars it sells, not just to the most expensive models.

Create a Bond

This is, of course, absolutely critical. The goal is to become the first offering your customers think of when they have a need your business can fulfill.

How do you do this?

By being there first: The first living being a baby goose sees when it is born, as Konrad Lorenz famously showed in his experiments, imprints that subject to them, even if that subject is a human being. The subject—despite not being a goose—becomes the mother to the younglings.

The same happens in business. 3M's Post-it brand sticky notes are an example. They were the first product of their type. Now, the 3M brand name is a stand-in for the category. Post-it notes means sticky notes, just as Kleenex means facial tissue.

By being there in a crisis.

By getting to know your customers and their needs.

By being consistent.

And by providing the human touch: empathy, understanding, courtesy, and reasonableness in your relations with customers will bond them to you and to your business.

A culture built on these values is a culture that echoes our ancestors' values.

Can an algorithm do that?

Create a Habit

Ideally, you don't need loyalty cards to create loyalty. Rather, you want customers to crave the intrinsic reward that comes from using your product or service.

I have worked out to the same album, *Moving Pictures*, by Rush for as long as I can remember. The album's mix of upbeat rhythms and lyrics shining a light on creativity, the excitement of cities, and a darkening political world just works for me. An elapsed time of about forty minutes, perfect.

The final track, "Vital Signs," winds down the album with a fading refrain lasting about a minute. As soon as that refrain starts, and especially when I hear the contrived word *evelate*, I know I'm in the home stretch of my workout, and I start to feel good about my accomplishment.

So it was pretty weird the other day, during the Era of Zoom, when I heard that refrain and thought to myself, "Hmmm, that workout went by fast. I must have been daydreaming."

I started to wind down my exercises and began putting away my gear. In the elevator I looked at my phone and realized I had been working out for just over twenty-five minutes.

"What the hell?" I thought. And then it dawned on me. I had inadvertently left my music player app on the random play setting. Sure enough I had. Mystery solved. I had worked out for just over half my usual workout time, but the refrain of that last song automatically signaled to me that I was done. That's the power of habit.

And so too Charles Duhigg has written a book under that very title. In it, the Pulitzer Prize–winning journalist lays out the simple pattern of a habit: stimulus—routine—reward.

For me that morning, I heard the refrain of "Vital Signs"—that was the stimulus— so without thinking, I began my routine of winding down my exercises and collecting my gear, and I felt the usual good feelings I get at the end of a workout for a job well done—that was the reward.

And all of this happened much earlier than it should have had I not had my music player on random play.

In *The Power of Habit*, Duhigg tells the story of how Pepsodent became the leading toothpaste, in the early twentieth century, because its unique ingredients not only gave the paste a fresh taste, but resulted in a cool, tingling feeling that users came to crave as the reward—the signal that their mouths were clean.

Duhigg pointed to what he calls keystone habits for their power to impact our behavior. These are habits like routine exercise, which have the power to spill over to other aspects of our lives, making us more likely to choose healthy foods and to temper our alcohol intake.

What pattern can you create for your offering to encourage customers' habitual usage? For example, hunger pang triggers the customer to order food from your establishment and delicious/healthy entrees arrive on time, every time.

Create Lock-in

Make it costly for customers to switch by creating lock-in:

- Penalty fees for ending a contract early
- Loss of ability or costs to transfer data
- Loss of familiarity with and trust in a product or service
- Loss of connectivity to other services your offering is integrated with
- Loss of selection, quality, reliability, or loyalty discounts
- Severed relationships with your friendly and expert team members whom your customers count on in good times and in bad

Notice that a number of these effects represent loss aversion, which we know is a more powerful psychological motivator than gaining something new.

The concept of lock-in—which is about the data—is the flip side of value created. It is the loss of that value, maybe to some really cool stuff, that keeps people in the club.

Spotify retains its users in a number of ways. I was astounded to learn that the service has more paying users (subscribers) and they are more profitable, according to

Rolling Stone who looked at their public books for 2019, than are the free, ad-supported users.

Ease of use is at the top of the reasons I suspect for the profitability of the service and for the high and loyal subscriber base. Ek, the founder, said to the interviewer at Stanford's ETL series his design approach is simple: "Make sure you are clear on the use case you are designing for, and build in the shortest route to get there."

In 2012, before the platform became ubiquitous, Ek said his design was aimed at three use-cases: "To play, to share, and to discover music."

When you use the service, you make playlists on your own or with friends so that now you have something you created, and therefore want to keep. That's a positive lock-in. The service was the first to allow a user to play any song on demand. That is an example of imprinting. The service delivers what the user wants each time, which creates a habit. You can take Spotify anywhere. It's free to play on many mobile platforms, and if you pay for the premium service, you can download songs, meaning an interruption in Wi-Fi or cell service does not mean silence. That's value.

When in doubt, figure out how to bring value and keep increasing the value you deliver to customers, and they will remain alongside you in the tent you have created.

Value and Pricing and Fees, Oh, My!

Coming up with a revenue model is too important a topic to bury in a paragraph or two.

So, first, what is a revenue model? Here are two excellent definitions:

- A revenue model describes who is going to pay your business for a specific good, service, or asset and how the price, rate, or fee will be determined.

- A revenue model is a framework for generating revenues. It identifies which revenue source to pursue, what value to offer, how to price the value, and who pays for the value. It is a key component of a company's business model.

The revenue model you develop and test and ultimately go with will be a reflection of you, your values, and your story. It will stem from your creative business idea.

The first choice for you to make will be deciding who is going to pay your business for a specific product, service, or asset. That sounds like a simple question and it is for many businesses. For a lot of new and innovative businesses, though, it is not.

Back to the question of who is going to pay your business (that is, which revenue source to pursue).

In the case of Google AdWords, the decision was clear. Advertisers were going to be the ones to pay. They would be the revenue source to pursue. Google could have chosen to charge people searching, or they could have chosen to charge both searchers and advertisers. We don't know if charging people to search would have worked, but we do know that *not* charging them to search did.

Think about this question in the context of some software revenue models. The internet culture walks to the beat of Free. This is the ethos of the early mass use of the internet, and you hear it drumming everywhere. I found it bewildering working in the immediate pull of Silicon Valley. Everybody, it seemed, wanted to give away their product entirely free, or at least with a free version, and then charge for a premium component.

But there is a downside to the mantra of free. That downside is that someone else has to provide the source of revenue. Most of the internet has decided that advertising—that advertisers—will be the source of revenue for their businesses.

Look at that sentence.

Someone is subsidizing all of your altruism because you are giving away your service at no charge. If it's not advertisers, it's your paying customers, the ones paying for premium services. Think about that for a minute. You are charging your most valued customers more than you need to because you want to make something available to the freeloaders for nothing. Does that make sense?

If it's not advertisers or sponsors paying for your business, or premium-paying customers, it might be in-app purchases.

Why do internet companies selling services want all those nonpaying users? The simple answer: to exploit them. Sorry. That's harsh. I should have said to leverage them. The users become the product, and the product is sold to advertisers and sometimes unwittingly.

As I write this, it also occurs to me that one of the reasons internet companies have offerings that are free is that free is hard to beat. Hmmm.

Whom to charge is an important consideration. For many internet businesses, increasing the number of users is in itself a goal to create a network effect (the "Hey, can you get a Facebook account so I can message you?") turning users and their information into the product to sell to advertisers.

The next part of the revenue model question is whether to charge a price, a rate, or a fee and on what basis will you charge: commission, per-unit price, subscription, or something else?

- A **price** usually connotes a one-time price that is subject to change. Most items purchased on Amazon sell at a fixed price.

- A **rate** is usually derived based on total percentages of an order or it could refer to a subscription rate. Your car rental price per day is a good example. Just make sure to bring the car back before the twenty-four-hour period expires.

- **Fees** are usually per service performed but can also be rates. Airlines are the kings of fees. "Oh, you want to bring luggage on your transatlantic flight. That'll be $50. Thank you." Real estate agents' fees are usually based on a percentage of the price, which is a great model for the agent especially when selling high-end properties.

The final question: How much will you charge for your services?

That can take some careful thinking. Look at alternatives from your customers' perspective. Think about the utility your customer derives. But never forget to test out your pricing with your intended users.

You could also do something like Alli Webb did with her mobile blowout service: "Just charge 'em forty bucks because that seemed about right and two twenties was just easy," she said to Guy Raz.

If your business is a service, it may be useful for you to think in terms of concrete products for a minute. It's ugly English to say it this way, but can you productize your service? That's verbacizing a noun. Ugh.

So, Service A, which for the sake of painting a picture is manicuring someone's nails, becomes: Basic Manicure, the premium version of which is Marvelous Manicure, and each product offers its own package of services. The quality level or degree of choice varies among the levels, and each service (product) is offered at a different price point.

Many services now offer three options: good, better, best. You can even nudge your customers to choose a level with handy little descriptors on your virtual or actual signage such as this: "Good, for those looking for a basic x," "Better, our most popular choice," or "Best, for when you deserve it all."

 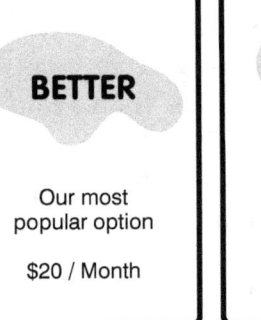 

PRICING OPTIONS WITH A NUDGE

I worked for a company that used this as a nudge—trust me, not many people want Good when they can plainly see that most people chose Better.

The concepts in psychology at play—in addition to nudge—which I am already borrowing here from behavioral economist Daniel Kahneman's book *Thinking, Fast and Slow*, are anchoring and framing.

Anchoring is the idea that people grab onto a number when it's mentioned early on in a negotiation or may consider an irrelevant or inaccurate adjacent price for a choice when making a product selection. If choosing the best level of service at $30 seems extravagant, I might feel okay choosing the most popular for $20.

Framing is also at work here in the three-choice example we are considering. Three levels of services are offered—none described as bad BTW—and one that advertises itself as the most popular. For most people—the 68 percent that fall within one standard deviation on a normal curve—the middle option is going to be alluring. If I want to be cheap, I go with the basic package, and if I want to really spoil myself—as in, "L'Oreal. Because you're worth it"—dammit, I'm going to go with the top choice.

A novel revenue model can also be a new way to compete. Take a look at what's out there and determine what similar businesses—if there are any—are doing now. Are there ways you can do it differently? For example, many traditional businesses are on a pay-as-you-go basis. Maybe you could create a subscription alternative to that (or vice versa).

Do research and see if most providers are charging piecemeal for their products. If so, you may be able to sell on a bundled basis. Maybe similar businesses are selling similar products at a similar price and competing on the basis of something else, like speed of delivery, availability, or reliability. Can you go higher or lower than the prevailing prices and create a premium or a discount offering? You get the picture.

We are seeing the software-as-a-service (SaaS) model spread to other industries. For example, private-planes-as-a-service, data-as-a-service, and, we will soon have artificial-intelligence-as-a-service.

In my house a popular service item is me. You have Doug-as-a-service.

My products are these:

> Duber (car service with a smile, door-to-door)
> Dugs (hugs)
> Doogle (ask me anything)

I don't charge a fee for my services. I have one customer, and that works just fine for me. She's a great supporter, my best friend, and the love of my life.

Your choice of revenue model is a reflection of your creative business idea. Choose wisely.

Reflect & Act

- A strong creative business idea will help you attract and retain customers. The more imaginative or original your ideas—the more your personality and personal story shines through in the execution of your business—the more attracted customers will be.

- Value delivered is key to your success. The greater the value you can create, the greater the value you can share with your customers, your investors, and yourself. Your revenue model choice and the amount you charge should follow from the value you create for customers and from the personal attributes you imbue in the business.

- Develop and test one customer acquisition method that works, and is profitable, before your first release if you can. Build retention into your design by how you talk about your business and share your story. Consider who will pay for your offering, in what way, and how much you will charge.

11
Build It and They Will Come

In some ways creating your first production release should be easy. You've already figured out what your solution, service, or production is and verified that it works (it does a job, solves a problem, fills a gap) and that customers would like to buy it. CLICK. So all you need to do now is the actual work of producing it.

In software, the first production release is the one after you have completed beta testing. The feature set is clear; the data architecture, sourcing, parsing, manipulating bits have been figured out; and the button is waiting to be pressed to go live. Yes, you will have bugs—but no worries—you have lots of bug swatters.

If your product is software, you no longer need to physically manufacture anything. There is no copying of your program on CD ROMS, no manuals or packaging to produce. After a week your first production release will be outmoded—replaced by your second production release. And so on.

If your product is a nuclear power plant, it doesn't work quite that way.

If your product is an automobile, it used to be the case that once the product shipped, you were done until the vehicle came into a dealer for service, but that too has changed. With so much software built into cars now, software updates are becoming more common. Tesla pushes software updates from the cloud to every car designated a recipient whenever they deem appropriate.

Consider these key questions about building your first production release:

- What will your first production release be?
- Who will build it, where will it be built and at what cost?
- In what quantities?

Who will build your product, provide your service, create your production? Where are those people? Do you need them to be on-site to deliver your offering to your customer, as most service businesses do, or can delivery be done remotely?

To get to your first production release, you need to have your design and production blueprints, raw materials, and steps in the recipe hard printed and in your hands. Your designs and processes will direct the most important people for the next part of your journey—the folks who create the designs, processes, and molds for the product, or fully develop the service or production you are creating.

Back to the critical discipline of manufacturing. If you are not a process/transfer engineer, I implore you to get—or hire—someone who is.

Here's the thing. Manufacturing a quality product, on time and to the quantities and cost levels needed—if it's a physical product—is as essential to your business as water is to ice cubes.

The service equivalent of quality manufacturing is quality service delivery. If your product is a creative production, then the equivalent of excellence in manufacturing is excellence in performance delivery.

As Reid Hoffman, a founder of LinkedIn and the podcast *Master of Scale*, would say, you need to perfect the customer experience before you scale.

Here's a way to think about culture: having a fantastic script for a TV series or film or Broadway is like having quality ingredients for a recipe. The words are essential. Having talented actors is like having a talented chef who can improvise as needed with those ingredients. Having talented cast members—and allowing them to improvise as necessary to go with the feel of the audience, or to absorb a new cast member—is the kind of agility you and your team will need to perform at high levels.

Here's what else I know.

The manufacturing of a product, or the delivery of a service or a performance, is the fruit of labor and ingenuity deployed well before the finished good can be enjoyed by someone—your customer or audience member. Raw materials have to be searched for and secured. The recipe needs to be tested and retested. Equipment may need to be ordered. People have to be trained.

When I worked in the corporate world, the manufacturing folks depended on us in marketing to figure out how much to make of each product and of each SKU. In turn, we depended on them. And, of course, flexibility is required in case a product demand forecast is wrong—scratch that—when the forecast turns out to be wrong. So the manufacturing folks need to plan for variances.

Here's something to figure out early on in your journey to bring your creative business idea to life. Figure out at least one way that you will build your first production release and cost it out—meaning, figure out how much it will cost to produce each unit at the initial volumes and at scale. Why? This will be essential when combined with the prices you intend to charge in determining how much money you will be able to make on a unit basis. Or go one step better, design to cost—meaning, pick the target cost first and let that drive product or service design and development.

Knowing what the managerial accounting wonks call unit margin may play a role in determining which customers you can serve and possibly where you may be able to disrupt a market. Knowing your costs is a basic piece of information you need to know, and it feeds into a basic profitability test for your business idea—one that people wanting to invest in you will want to know.

Figuring out a pathway to your finished product is an essential challenge every entrepreneur must meet. Figuring out how to do so efficiently and reliably is essential as you move from early prototype, to prerelease, to first commercial release, to scaled product. Can you drive costs lower via material, process changes, volume, or efficiencies gained in the electronics?

Where are you going to produce? Will you go offshore? Yes, Asia in general is a low-cost area in which to produce goods, especially if your volumes are high and thus giving you leverage with your supplier. If you haven't done it before, take the time to find reliable suppliers. Use word of mouth to locate suppliers if you can, which may be the best way to ensure a good supplier.

Whichever way you decide to go for the production of your offering, build in some redundancy.

If you are going to cross a crocodile-infested raging river that is rushing toward a massive waterfall, and you're in a motorboat, it's best to make sure you have two engines, lots of gas, and an experienced pilot.

Ready, Set, Release

Do you know when your favorite Christmas—sorry, winter holiday—blockbuster is coming out? I thought so. What about the next season of a favorite streaming series? I thought so again. I personally could not wait for the final season of *Game of Thrones* to drop. And then it did, and I am still trying to put it behind me. I think they should redo it. But that's not the point.

The point is, your customers, or at least some of your customers, should be eagerly awaiting the release of your solution—whatever your solution is. Unless you want to do a soft launch, which to me sounds like an oxymoron.

How can something be launched softly? If you need a big launch from day one, a soft launch is out of the question. Rockets—businesses that have to go big from day one—cannot be launched softly. But some businesses can be launched softly, like a boat. Picture it—a canoe—being released on a quiet lake, gently sliding into the fog at dawn heralded by the eerie call of a loon. That can be a launch too, no? You can start gently, create a rhythm, and build from there. Your canoe can become a giant canoe, with many paddlers, or maybe a canoe armada.

Pilot launches are an example of a soft launch where your product or service is evaluated by a particular customer or group to see if it works and meets their objectives.

Now is the time to go back to all of the people you have been involving in the early version testing and improvement, to the folks who may have tested some of your branding or packaging or messaging, and with whom you CLICKed:

- Let them know of your impending first release, and,
- Involve them in your campaign to build anticipation for the first release.

This is essential.

You spent time with customers, lab (technical) people, investors, creators, and key opinion leaders in the development of your offering. Now is the time to continue building and leveraging those relationships. CLICK.

Put the serene lake out of your mind now and bring up a pachinko machine. If you've never seen a pachinko machine, picture a vertical pinball machine. As a player, you purchase balls from the machine and shoot them into the playing area just as you would a pinball—though in pachinko the balls are smaller and you often have more than one ball in play at a time (you can have more than one ball in play with pinball, too, but I don't recommend it).

As the balls fall by the force of gravity, and career from brass pin to brass pin, some end up in catchers, which is superb because that gives the player still more balls to play with. Some of the balls, however, fall to the bottom and are lost. The object of pachinko is to catch as many balls as possible. The balls can be exchanged for prizes such as a stuffed Godzilla.

Potential customers are like pachinko balls. Some will fall right through the playing field of your business, not even aware you exist; others will bounce around on a few pins and may come close to your catchers, and then fall off; still others will land in your catchers—and bingo—oops no one says bingo in a pachinko parlor—how about, "Pachinko, I got more pachinko balls!"

Like pachinko balls, potential customers may first become aware of your offering before becoming interested, leading to trial use—evaluation—and possibly repeat use and loyalty.

For the launch of your first production release, your goal is adoption by the people you are trying to attract. So what do you do? Unless you're selling water on the Great Wall of China on a hot day, your customers first have to have heard something about you before they become interested. What can you do before the release of your product or service to get more people excited about the upcoming release of your offering?

When I worked in the corporate world, we aimed for 80 percent aware-of-and-intend-to-try on day one among our closest and most influential customers. For the next tier of customers, the goal was 60 percent aware-of-and-intend-to-try our offering. This takes a lot of work, but it focuses the troops prior to launch on a goal and really helps with the early days of your business—just make sure if you manage to create anticipation that you can meet the demand. What you want is to become that restaurant that nobody goes to because it's too crowded.

Here are some ways you can increase awareness and intent to use:

- Email list announcement
- Social media
- Advertising
- Signage
- Blog posts
- PR (print, radio, or podcast)
- Website
- Video announcements or YouTube channel
- Classic, for example, a countdown clock on your website, a coming soon sign
- Creative (What else can you do to create anticipation for your offering?)

At Everbooked, the software start-up I was part of, we made sure to capture the email addresses of any interested party that came into our orbit. Capturing email addresses and getting the okay to use them in the prelaunch phase and beyond is essential to any business.

Seth Godin, the prolific blogger, entrepreneur, and educator, wrote an entire book on the subject. In *Permission Marketing: Turning Strangers into Friends and Friends into*

Customers, Godin explained why people don't look at ads anymore and how you can build a relationship with intended customers, and sell to them effectively, if you just get their permission. See, Mom was right, you never can say *please* or use your manners often enough.

Building a list of interested parties before your first production release means you have people ready and willing to step up from day one. Just be sure to be courteous, professional, interesting, and relevant. Make sure you don't spam them with every little detail that might be of interest to you. Put yourself in their shoes and tell them what's in it for them. Make it simple. Appeal to their needs and their point of view.

And be sure to have an easy, hassle-free opt-out link. Nothing makes a consumer angrier than if you do not provide an escape hatch. Maybe they landed on your email list inadvertently to start with, or the content you are providing them—or your offering—may no longer be relevant. Who knows? Actually, it doesn't really matter why they want to opt out, as long as you make it easy for them to do so.

Once they hit the escape button, they may click on a couple buttons to explain why, but don't push your luck. I know, because I've heard from angry customers looking to be let go and seeing no way out. They give you permission to engage with them, as long as they can pull the escape hatch lever at any time as good form and the CAN-SPAM act dictates.

A similar concept exists with any of your social media pages. People will follow and unfollow you at will. Keep it interesting and real, and you will build your following over time. Using social media is a powerful way to build awareness and intent to use for your offering.

Before you release your first production version, you can build a name for yourself by creating a website and by blogging on the topic. A website today is like a calling card in the past. It is essential for virtually all businesses in the public sphere—and most in the private sphere.

Basic websites are easy to create and maintain. It's worth learning the basics of how to create a website. If you don't have the capacity or interest in doing so yourself, pay someone to create one for you. The language and terminology used for your website should include keywords to search for your product or service. Worth mentioning again, research "What is SEO?" (search engine optimization) to learn more. The idea is for customers and those interested in your business to find you easily on the web in your little slice of heaven that is the part of the world you are staking your claim within.

Another plug for blogging. Blogging is an excellent way to show your expertise and to create awareness and excitement for your coming offering, and to be found by people searching on the web.

A blog a colleague and I wrote for the software start-up in California I was a part of was a very strong reason our business rose to the top of the search results in our category. Writing about your business, in language your customers use, I can attest, attracts those same customers to your website. It's a natural form of search engine optimization (SEO).

Blogging is a fantastic way to let your personality shine through, too, which, after all, is what you are trying to do with your creative business idea. What you write on your blog will bring people in and allow you to tell your story and create interest in your offering.

Once there on your blog, people will look for interesting items to engage with, including information about your upcoming release and a sign-up form so they can be notified as soon as it's ready.

Try to direct people through to your website by asking them to leave you their email address. A simple web form is all you need, which could be gathered by making some of your collateral—like a white paper or a consultation—available free to people who complete your web form. On your website, or with a physical sign, let people know what is coming and approximately when—set up and maintain a countdown clock to your release date.

Build more catchers in your pachinko machine by blogging, creating a website, and capturing names for your email list using webforms.

Build it and they will come—especially if they are excited about your coming offering. There's so much you can do to create anticipation for the first release of your offering.

While the folks building your offering or creative production are busy building and producing, you can be out in the world with a giant paintbrush painting every billboard, park bench, and virtual brick building with your message: "Coming soon, something you just gotta see."

Reflect & Act

- If a new business opens and nobody is there to enjoy it, did it make a sound? You've spent a lot of time, energy, and ingenuity getting from concept all the way to finished product. Spend some time making sure people know about your product, are anticipating its arrival, and will know how to get it from day one.

- The product, service, or production you bring forward for your initial release sets an impression and possibly a trajectory for your business. Spend the time to make sure you can meet demand and the expectations of your early customers. Celebrate them when they arrive.

12
Ten, Nine, Eight ...

There are only two kinds of launches. (Have you noticed I like to see the world in twos, like Noah?) A boat launch and a rocket launch. A boat launch is more like a release than a launch.

A rocket launch says, "All eyes on us, there's going to be a countdown, some thrusters will fire, and a massive, shiny new vessel with our insignia on it is going to try to break the earth's gravity. Oh, and something might go wrong. It's going to be thrilling."

A boat release is gentle. You pick the body of water to launch in, the time of day, and determine whether there is fog in the air. The environment is contained.

The body of water represents a specific group of customers—it's land-locked. If you want to, you can launch just one boat in one body of water, or more than one boat in more than one body of water.

Boats are cheap compared to rockets.

Picture a rocket poised to take off, staged and ready to go. "All systems go," says the mission director, once all the checks have been completed to their satisfaction.

The readiness of a rocket is an apt metaphor in the SPARK-CLICK-GO world where the trigger for the GO decision, the launch decision, is pressed once your prerelease or first-release version has CLICKed with your intended customers and with at least one person from each of the other essential audiences:

- Customers
- Lab (technical) people
- Investors
- Creators
- Key opinion leaders

This is especially true if you are doing a conventional launch (a rocket launch). If you are doing a boat launch, you can be a little more chill—just a little.

NASA is famous for checklists, steps that must be taken, systems that must be fully functioning before hitting the GO button and igniting the rocket engines.

Here's a checklist for your launch:

- Will your product, service, or creative production be ready on time and be of high quality for your launch? Are your distributors/distribution platforms primed and ready?

- Have customers and opinion leaders been talking about your upcoming product/service/production? Do you have traction with a small group of customers trying out your prerelease version, or do you have a partnership deal to announce?

- Do all the people on your team know the launch plan, and have they been trained for their role in making it happen?

- Do you have a customer support plan in place?

- Have you notified the press, customers, suppliers, partners, supporters/investors, and other stakeholders?
- Do you have contingency plans for possible derailments or hiccups (bad weather, a pandemic, a shortage of supplies, for example)?

And here are methods of launching your offering:

- *All Hands on Deck* (everyone that is part of your team, and part of your support team—officially and unofficially—to be called to get the word out about your launch)
- *Hit the Ground Running* (fulfill preorders and implement your most effective customer acquisition method: direct sales, Facebook or Google ads, in-person sampling)
- *Roll 'em* (creation of engaging videos to announce your launch—these are shareable on all channels including social media, to your email list, to bloggers or media, and on your website for inbound traffic)
- *Just Hit Send* (email announcement to listserv)
- *Full Court Press* (press release on the wire)
- *Red Carpet* (event with press invited)
- *PSST, Just for You* (giving exclusive access to handpicked media/bloggers in advance of release)
- *First Past the Post* (blog post)
- *Tell All Your Friends* (social media posts)
- *Try it, You'll Like It* (create a trial offer)

- *Get Yours Now* (there is not a line people can avoid, create a waiting list like Tesla did for its Model 3 and Robinhood did for its no-commission trading platform)

- *If You Love Us Tell the World* (and if you hate us, tell us, we'll make it right: call for reviews)

- *Call an Audible* (last-minute play called on the line of scrimmage because of some change on the field—all football jargon)

- *Kick-Off Rally* (an internal event to rally the troops)

FIRST RELEASE AVAILABLE, GET YOURS NOW

GrowthHit is an online growth marketing company out of Seattle that helps clients design the perfect digital marketing funnel. The firm touts on their blog the short-video format as crucial for launching, creating trial offers, and developing a wait list of eager customers anxious to buy your product once it launches.

Neil Patel wrote a nice post, too, on his self-named traffic blog (also) offering seven things we can learn about inspirational product launches from Steve Jobs.

I like Patel's observation that Jobs kept it real in his legendary Apple launches by talking about the impact on people the company's tech would have, rather than discussing gigahertz and megabytes.

Patel points out that it helps to be revolutionary with your ideas and create products your customers will talk about, as well as the importance of getting opinion leaders involved early. Indeed, launch days or launch events are really the culmination of work you have done to ready the audience for the show.

As I was writing this section of my book on a beautiful day in Boston in 2020, an article popped into my email feed via SmartBrief, an email newsletter about start-ups I have been receiving for years and happily recommend.

SmartBrief alerted me to a blog post by Joe Procopio on builtin. In it, the self-proclaimed multi-exit, multi-failure COO of Precision Fermentation—yes, he helps make better beer (!)—writes about the importance of targeting publicity to people who can make a difference to your start-up, timed to evidence of traction.

I love the headlines he suggests for any press release you should be able to write before you launch:

> ABC Company Announces the Launch of XYZ Product: Company comes out of beta with 100 paying customers
>
> ABC Company Announces the Launch of XYZ Product: Company partners with MegaCorp on nationwide distribution deal
>
> ABC Company Announces the Launch of XYZ Product: Company touts a proven 50 percent savings in widget production costs

Joe writes: "Launch quietly until you have traction."

When you launch, you want to be serving those customers who are going to be the most valuable in helping you shape your market. He says, "You have a hand in selecting this valuable customer segment: It's those customers who you believe will find the most value in your product. Find them and sell to them first."

He's an advocate of the slow and quiet release—the boat launch—until traction is built with a small and selective group of important customers—and then, and maybe only then, the rocket release.

To paraphrase Bill Creelman, the founder of the Massachusetts-based beverage company Spindrift, speaking on the *How I Built This* podcast: We knew we were ready to GO when we finally figured out a way to flavor our seltzer water naturally without our product degrading during shipping.

One of the best launch examples I can think of in the popular culture of late is the Tesla Model 3. Picture a large dark stage. The crowd (mostly males I notice) is enthralled, smartphones are rolling, flashlights are on—it looks like a concert. Elon Musk is talking about his latest—limited release hit—the Model 3 from Tesla.

This is July 2017. Musk tells folks in the audience their car should be ready for them in about a year and a half. Some of the audience—the really early birds on the list—will drive off in their Model 3 that night, and several cars are lined up in rows to one side.

This is the model that people paid $1,000 for the privilege of being on a preorder list—deposits that became working capital for the company.

If you can get people so aligned with your mission that they will come to a car launch to be told, hey, wait a year and half and it will be here, you must be doing something right.

Imagine Drake inviting you to a concert, putting up a PowerPoint with a few pics from the studio, or sitting around the kitchen table writing songs, rapping a few bars from his new material, and maybe showing you some sheet music—saying, hey, come back in a year, it's going to be a helluva show. Oh, and I know you're having issues with our current stuff, don't worry we're trying to fix it. And yet you're enthralled somehow.

It's a bit cultish but Musk was not just making promises, he was delivering on a promise the company made many years prior to bring a cool and affordable electric car to market.

Musk and company generated about 450,000 preorders for the Model 3. The feat is all the more impressive when you realize the Model 3 is a sedan, and the sedan segment of the market has been nudged off the road in the recent decade because of shifting driver preference for SUVs and crossovers.

When I think of the Tesla example, and successful launches I have been a part of, I see two patterns: The first is all about the value you are bringing to your customers through the use of imaginative or original ideas. The second is around the importance of your story and the mission you are on with your business idea.

A story that reflects something that is unique about you and about what you are working to bring to the world attracts people to you. If you can get that kind of passion across to others, and make it important or interesting, they will want to be part of your mission. They will identify with you, and they will be eager to be at the unveiling of your first (and your next) big thing.

Once you've launched, and even before as we have seen in the Elon Musk example, an entrepreneur needs to always be sharing their story and the value of their products enthusiastically. Let's call it ABS. Always be sharing. Always be selling.

Storytelling is an essential element to bringing your creative business idea to life.

Do You Want to Know How to Make a Million Dollars?

I started my professional career in sales, a skill by the way that is highly useful as an entrepreneur. Either you, or someone else on your team—but usually you and other people—will need sales skills to raise money, to attract partners, and to attract customers.

In Silicon Valley, they use the term *hustler*. I have to admit the first time I heard that term I was perplexed. Hustler just felt dirty to me—a hustler was someone who suckered people into betting money playing pool. Another term used in Silicon Valley is *growth hacker*. A growth hacker sounds like a euphemism for an arborist, but in the Valley, where business is just done differently, it means a marketer who can grow your user base using internet savvy and programming skills.

When I was offered a sales role—my first real job after college—with Bristol Myers, my dad told me that sales was a superb starting place in business. He said, "Doug, sales is the lifeblood of every business. If you can sell, you will always have a job, or you can run your own business."

My first manager, Curt Carlson, was a fine boss and a professional salesperson. I learned a lot from him starting the first time he joined me on a work-with—a day during which he would ride along to all of the sales calls I had planned. Before each sales call we talked about the objectives, and after each call we would debrief. It was arduous but it worked. Here's the scene in my car after a particular sales call failed to go well:

Curt: "Doug, how do you think that call went?"

Doug: "Hmmm, not too bad. He seemed to like some of our products and wanted samples."

Curt: "True, but did you notice he didn't want to engage around our new product? Do you want to know how to gain someone's interest early on?"

Doug: "Sure." (Duh, what other answer could I have given?)

Curt: "What's your reaction if I ask you something like: Doug, would you like to know how to make a million dollars?"

Doug: "Absolutely. Tell me more. I would probably say. Oh wait, ah I see what you're trying to do. Ya, that would work—thanks, that is helpful."

I would later learn—and remember—that the opening had a name in the sales world. It was called a statement of purpose and tentative benefit. It works for elevator calls and openings with lots of people you may want to involve in your business, including investors and prospective customers.

I learned a solid definition of sales from Curt too. He was the first person who lived by the definition that sales, or more precisely selling, was really just a transfer of enthusiasm. If you think about it, that is true. When you have bought into something, I mean really bought into it, you will be enthusiastic. Your enthusiasm will come naturally.

So, too, will your enthusiasm come naturally as an entrepreneur with a creative business idea because that idea, by definition, will be a reflection of you and your values. Selling will be easier, or may come naturally to you, because you will be transferring your enthusiasm for the idea you want to bring to life with other people.

Once you have enthusiastic customers, you will need to support them.

One of the things Joe Gebbia and Brian Chesky learned early on with their creative business idea, AirBedandBreakfast, was that hosts usually uploaded pretty basic photos representing their places. This reflected not only on the hosts, but on the platform. Gebbia and Chesky thought they could improve this image by providing professional photos of people's pads.

In the beginning, when the platform only had a handful of listings in New York City, the founders did the photography themselves. Gebbia and Chesky had been students at the

Rhode Island School of Design so they had an eye for composition and lighting. When they were maxing out on their credit cards to fund their fledgling venture, doing the photography themselves was the cheapest way to get it done. The pro shots increased income, made the hosts happier, and made the platform look more professional.

It may have been one of the single most important acts the pair did to support their customers and improve their platform after launch—when people were curious, but skeptical, about sleeping in strangers' homes.

The SPARK-CLICK-GO Journey has been designed to build momentum. You've come a long way from the SPARK of your idea through the testing and developing of your idea. Once you launch your offering, it's time to get out there to sell and support it. It's GO time.

Reflect & Act

- What kind of launch will you choose? The slow, controlled sort, like a boat launch, or the all-or-nothing rocket launch? If you choose a rocket launch, have you ensured that all systems are ready before you press GO?

- Once you launch, things shift—you've got to be ready to support your customers and make sure you are delivering on whatever promises you made to yourself and to them.

- Are you ready to always be sharing the story of your enterprise and the value you offer: how you got the idea, what need in the market you are filling, what value your offering brings, what your mission is?

13
Go Forth and Multiply

Hundreds of robots work in unison to build a car as it slinks its way through an assembly path in a massive, brightly lit factory. Workers in lab coats and safety glasses move like ants as they serve each steel beast, passing its hulk among them as they finish their tiny task.

A factory building cars is a typical image that pops to mind when you or I think of automation, but factory automation is not what I mean when I say automation.

The kind of automation I'm referring to is more mundane: tasks like capturing email addresses of people interested in your business, automatic generation of invoices, posting cash receipts to your income statement. Stuff like that. Ordering supplies when they become low, scheduling your weekly meeting, collecting survey data and sending it as a report, autogenerated communications to prospects depending on an action they take in relation to your business. These are the things that every business can do more of to make the business run more efficiently and capture more value.

Here's a way to think about automation:

PHYSICAL DOMAIN	PROCESS DOMAIN	COGNITIVE DOMAIN
Augment/Replace Manual Tasks	Augment/Replace Information-Rich Tasks	Augment/Replace Thinking Tasks

WHAT OPPORTUNITIES FOR AUTOMATION ARE RIGHT FOR YOUR CREATIVE BUSINESS IDEA?

I have ordered countless items on Amazon. (Well, not really, Amazon can easily count the number of items I have ordered.) Maybe you have too. Have you ever talked with a person at Amazon? I have never spoken to a carbon-based life form at Amazon. Yet, somehow, I am quite happy with my overall experience at Amazon.

I am a repeat customer who does not really recommend Amazon to friends—Amazon hardly needs me to make my friends want to try Amazon—but I do find myself saying, "I found it on Amazon," or "You might find it on Amazon." So I am talking up the company more than enough.

Most of the entire experience from an Amazon customer's viewpoint—and much of the logistics—are done in an automated fashion. When Jeff Bezos set out to create a store with everything, his vision included a ton of software and intelligent hardware to make it happen.

From the moment I land on Amazon's site, through my search, selection, and payment process, I am guided on a seamless tour. The system confirms my order (or allows me to cancel), tells me when the item has shipped, notifies me of its progress like it was the next coming, and, presto, the package arrives on my doorstep. If I need to reverse the process, that, too, is pretty easy—all without a human in sight except the UPS or Amazon delivery driver, and their days are numbered. Enter drones.

What can you do in your business to create a smooth customer experience your customers will value?

The first part of that answer probably has to do with software. Regardless of your creative business idea, you can make some part of it—the search, the purchase, the delivery, the rating—seamless for, and therefore valued by, your customer.

How do you decide if you need the human touch and in which parts of your business? Probably in fewer places than you think.

One of the places you may want to keep a human on guard may be in answering the phone. Depending on the size of your business, this can bring a personal touch people will appreciate. But do you really need a human answering the phone? Can you bake in an automated system your customers will love like a smooth website that leads to human contact seamlessly when needed? If so, do it.

You need not build everything either. Tools are out there for almost any business to adapt, and many will provide payment plans to grow with your business.

Take Toast in the restaurant business, for example. Toast offers a point-of-sale terminal and handheld point-of-sale devices so wait staff can bring the payment right to diners' tables—something available in other countries for years and curiously only now catching on in the States. The company provides seamless online ordering as well as a payroll and staff management solution all-in-one with pricing plans made to order.

Customers start for a thousand bucks and then pay a reasonable monthly subscription fee. That's fairly inexpensive compared to hiring someone to build and maintain a custom system. The result? A business that's easier to run and a better experience for guests, and all this for a small cash layout.

As with many situations, you can choose to buy or build. Buying—or more likely renting—will often be the way to go unless you have surplus software programming capability.

For example, if you want to create an online shop, you can readily do so using Shopify. If you need a way for your customers to pay online for your services, you can plug Stripe into your website—done. Similarly, for marketing and sales automation, there is HubSpot. For HR there is BambooHR or Gusto. For customer support there is Zendesk. You name the function, there is an offering ready for you. So plug in, simplify, and automate.

Here are two examples of businesses using data and automation in the context of customer satisfaction.

It cost me $400 to rent a video of *Kill Bill*. Want to know why?

Netflix, you may remember, once had a video-by-mail service. Delivering DVDs to people's homes was how Netflix disrupted what Blockbuster did, which was rent videos from their stores. You may know the story. Reed Hastings was famously pissed off about paying overdue fees at Blockbuster, so he made sure there were no overdue fees for his mail order DVD customers.

I had a subscription to the DVD mail service with Netflix for a long time and, as with a lot of subscriptions, I forgot I had it. I was paying for the DVD service and for the streaming service. So I was paying $7.99 a month for the DVD part of my service for three and half years while no longer receiving DVDs by mail, and I had forgotten to return *Kill Bill*.

Netflix, as with most tech companies, is built by programmers who are adept at creating algorithms to recommend new streaming content to users. Yet, Netflix never told me I was overdue three and a half years with *Kill Bill*. Are you telling me that Netflix could not have flagged my overdue rental? All they had to say was, "Hey, Mr. Ross, we've noticed you've had *Kill Bill* in your possession for three and a half years, have you finished watching it yet? Maybe you want to return it?"

Funny how Netflix couldn't have their bots flag my account when they are fully capable of giving me recommendations all the time on content to watch.

When I spoke to a customer service rep about all of this, solving the mystery as to why *Kill Bill* cost me nearly $400 (in monthly payments for the DVD service I was not using), she offered me two things. One was empathy. The second: I could keep the *Kill Bill* video.

Subscription businesses love this stuff—dormant accounts hooked to even more dormant account holders' credit cards for which the company is providing zero service. A slang or trade name for this type of dormant account may exist. Ping me if you know one. I'm going to call them *Kill Bill* accounts. I promptly canceled the DVD by mail part of my subscription that Netflix had looked the other way on for three and a half years. I was really ticked off, but I have this anecdote to tell, so it's not a total loss.

Still this is kinda ironic don't ya think in the context of Reed Hastings, Netflix's founder, being ticked off at Blockbuster for charging him overdue fees, and then deciding he had a better model?

"Revenge is a dish best served up cold." Thank you, Mr. Tarantino. That is inspiring. I should write Mr. Hastings a little nastygram or send him a copy of this book.

The second example of company automation working well is this one. This is simple. During the COVID-19 crisis, I wondered aloud to my wife, Bridget: "Hmmm, we are hardly driving our cars right now, honey, I wonder if our insurance company will automatically give us a discount?"

She took my annoyance in stride and said, "Oh, right. Like that'll happen. Honestly, hon, it's probably not worth you spending time wondering about."

I'm lucky. She keeps me grounded.

I had forgotten this exchange when a few weeks later I got a notification from GEICO saying they had automatically reduced my premiums during the pandemic. Bingo. That's what I'm talking about.

Score: Geico 1 Netflix 0

You pick the winner.

Ever try to buy clothes for an important woman in your life or for yourself (if you are a woman)? It's not so easy.

That's the problem Katrina Lake wanted to solve when she entered the retail business. She thought computer algorithms might be the ideal shoppers to help women buy clothes. Algorithms get to know what a woman wants. They never forget what she has already bought. And their feelings are never hurt when she returns an item that they sent her.

Algorithms happen to scale nicely too. So if Lake was going to pull off mass personal shopping, these little bits of code, properly nourished with the right data, could work with one woman at a time, or with millions.

Stitch Fix is Lake's creative business idea. It's her way of marrying human curation with data to meet her customers' tastes, needs, and lifestyles. Stitch Fix's mission is to change the way people find clothes they love by combining technology with the personal touch of seasoned style experts.

The Stitch Fix experience is not merely curated—it's truly personalized to each shopper. The company's staff and robots are ready to help style seekers save time, look great, and evolve their look over time.

Picture a personal clothes shopper. They are stylists who love fashion, know their store's inventory, and get to know each of their customers so well they can recommend the perfect outfit for an occasion or for a particular look. Our imaginary personal shopper is terrific, but they are expensive so only the high-level stores—the ones with fat margins—can afford to provide personal shoppers.

When Lake worked as an investment banker, she saw that no one was doing a good job of harnessing data to bring a better buying experience to millions. She saw a chance to create the Netflix of online clothes retailing. In the process she's been creating the future of retail—the data-driven fashion business.

Here's how it works. Customers enter the Stitch Fix site, create a profile by answering questions about their preferences, needs, and sizing, and, voila, they're ready to go. Customers order and receive fixes—the company's name for orders. The cost? Twenty bucks a hit, oops sorry, twenty bucks a fix. (The twenty gets credited to customers' orders if they keep any of the selections in the fix.) Sweet. For $49 a customer can ride all year, theoretically ordering a fix a day, trying on all the clothes and sending everything back, postage paid, all covered by the annual fee.

Stitch Fix's data funnels collect each customer's behavior—and the collective behaviors of all customers. While Lake and team are not trying to build a perpetual motion machine, the recommendation engines will evolve and become smarter over time. There will be an experience effect that will likely make the company better able to survive and thrive.

According to Lauren Smiley of Fast Company, some of the machine-learning advances have come in big leaps. In 2017 Stitch Fix's Chris Moody, an astrophysicist, created a feature called Style Shuffle, which allows customers to rate a set of clothes each day. This has resulted in a Carl Sagan number (billions and billions) of training points—a massive training set—for the company's algorithms.

The journey to take Stitch Fix public was full of surprises for Lake. As she told *Inc.* magazine, recalling one investor who did not take her seriously: "Your business is on fire, your team is great, but I just don't feel passionate about women's apparel."

Lake hopes Stitch Fix's success will prompt VCs to—as she puts it diplomatically—reexamine their mental filters. "At least I know the capitalist part of the venture capitalists will be regretful of the decisions they've made," she said.

Lake said she is passionate about helping women achieve confidence daily. She founded Stitch Fix to help women everywhere discover and explore their style through a truly client-focused shopping experience. The company's nearly 4,000 stylists, 600 brands, and algorithms hooked to an IV of data help to create the kind of human-filtered precision needed to provide personal styling at scale.

Lake cultivates a culture, too, that straddles the boundaries of human and silicon intelligence. Smiley says Lake strives to recruit bright and kind software programmers and tasks them with working on a real problem with a merchandiser or stylists as part of her selection process.

Did Lake and company solve the problem of buying clothes for women?

According to Smiley's reporting: "The company [in 2019] recorded its highest-ever rate of purchased items per fix among female customers in its most recent earnings, indicating that all that data science and personalization is paying off."

The company was profitable as early as 2014 and has achieved a peak market cap north of $5 billion. In 2019, Stitch Fix engaged more than three million customers.

It looks like Stitch Fix has cracked the nut of figuring out what clothes to buy for women. The company is so good at that, they've expanded to men's fashion and beyond.

This is a SPARK-CLICK-GO success story. First, the idea was worth pursuing. It was a creative business idea, the timing was right, the team was strong, it did not have a fatal flaw.

The SPARK was to bring data science to retail women's fashion. The CLICK was a model that worked with the five essential audiences. When Lake and team decided to GO, they went big—they were ready to scale, grow, and get better because growth and improvement was purpose-built into the fabric of their idea.

Some benefits of automation (like the Stitch Fix success) are these:

- Makes scaling easier
- Recordkeeping logs—company memory
- Nondiscriminatory (if you deploy algorithms make sure they have consciously been designed to remove bias)
- Less expensive
- Meet expectations for how a lot of customers like to interact with businesses
- Fewer cash dealings
- Reduce head count needs
- Flexes with volume changes in demand and supply

The more you automate, the more you will be able to scale. So consider the scalability of any system you develop or deploy to run your business. Give some thought to what your business may become in the future, not only to the immediate needs you have.

And then there are some risks of automation:

- Not personal—may turn off some customers
- Costs may be high
- May not work for your situation

You should not automate any element of your business where a human can better deliver value to your customer. If you have a massage business, it's the expertise and touch of the masseuse, the therapeutic benefits, and the overall experience that your customers are paying for.

If you're a small shop and you have an elaborate inbound phone menu, that might tick people off more than the time saving it creates—especially if people truly value access to you and your front-line providers for their expertise, human empathy, and wisdom.

Remember that automation of some customer functions—for example, online shopping—may be preferred for some of your customers, and not for others. Automation may become an option—one channel for people who love your offering to access—but don't chuck your stand-alongside human channel without serious forethought.

Keep It Real

Keep anything that is core to your creative business idea. If your CBI is creating handmade wedding cakes, don't automate the making of the cakes. If your CBI is one-on-one coaching sessions for women executives with women mentors, don't automate that. If your CBI includes any promise of human delivery, make sure to keep it real—keep it human.

Except for core human elements essential to your offering, all else should be considered for automation. Do it right, and you can build an efficient business for today, one that is scalable for tomorrow.

Here's something else to think about: One person's business need is another person's business.

To you it's a process to automate—for providers of automation for that process, it's their whole business. They've already thought about it and built the tools—they live and breathe that process. These folks get super excited about automating payrolls. Why not take advantage of all that know-how and enthusiasm and pick a system that works for your business? Most likely they will run the software, too—you won't need to load it on your systems, and you can start with a small, maybe even a free, plan. This is the law of comparative advantages writ small. Take advantage of the strengths of others so you can concentrate on your own.

The costs of automating are negligible for a ton of the mundane office processes you may need. This is different if your business is creating a new manufacturing system for electric scooters. For that the cost will be high, but so too are the benefits.

AI is already part of some automation.

Did you know you can already insert artificial intelligence into the way you do things? *Harvard Business Review*, in 2018, predicted that AI would "make the greatest impact in marketing services, supply chain management, and manufacturing," according to a blog post of the university's Extension School. The post points to healthcare and data transparency and security as burgeoning use-cases for artificial intelligence.

Mark Esposito, PhD, director of the Nexus FrontierTech and an instructor of Harvard's Artificial Intelligence in Business: Creating Value with Machine Learning course is quoted saying, "For companies looking to leverage AI, the first step is to look at which parts of your current operations can be digitized. Rather than dreaming up a magic-bullet solution, businesses should consider existing tech that can free up resources or provide new insights."

Dr. Esposito explains that problems must be narrowly defined in order for AI to play a role. AI is already helping businesses with better chat services, help for the visually impaired, personalized advertising, fraud detection, and predicting consumer behavior. AI is used to make recommendations for the next streaming show for you to enjoy.

AI and machine learning—or the ability for computers to find matches among massive amounts of data after learning from a sample set—can help your business.

I heard the phrase "data is the new oil" recently. That certainly applies to the new reality. What data can you harness in your business? Can you develop algorithms to make better and better recommendations for products your business sells online, or can you have AI figure out the most likely customers to target with an online ad?

It's easy to see a scalable business when it has already been built. Starbucks is obviously a scalable business—there is a store on every corner. But was that obvious back in the early days when Howard Schultz was thinking about whether and how to grow? Retail stores and restaurants in general are easy to scale. There's a pattern there called franchising. Or you can take a company-owned growth approach. Or you can use a hybrid approach.

Broadway shows at one point were not scalable—now there are traveling companies.

Concerts were once thought to be nonscalable. The pathway was well trodden: do a show in every major city—or cities where you could book a gig—when you had new material. That has been broken with the advent of in-house residency gigs for big acts like Celine Dion in Vegas. Cirque du Soleil scaled somewhat too. It was much tougher to scale a circus when you had elephants, tigers, and unusual humans as part of the act. Not that everyone can swing upside down from their feet, but there are enough people out there with gymnastic abilities and entertainment flare who can be trained for parts in the latest Cirque du Soleil show.

You've heard, no doubt, "It is just as easy to fall in love with a rich person as it is a poor one, so you might as well marry rich." It might just as accurately be said: "It's just as easy to go into a scalable business as it is a nonscalable business, so you might as well go for the scalable one."

Would it be just as easy to scale creative or original ideas that deliver value for others profitably, while uniquely reflecting and benefiting its creators? Maybe, maybe not, but it's worth thinking about before you walk down the aisle.

Why is being able to scale important?

Depending on your goals, scalability—ouch that's kind of an ugly twenty-first-century word—is important.

Remember, you may never want to scale your business, but making it scalable might be the smartest move you make.

To scale is to grow. To scale is to reach more people with your business—that could tie nicely into your personal mission to bring value to people in an expressive way. To scale is to attract (certain) key people to your business such as employees, partners, investors, media, and many people you will not be able to predict.

To scale is to return more profits on your investment of blood, sweat, and fears.

Here are some components to look for when thinking about scale:

- Product or service can be produced at large quantities—production is flexible.

- People delivering your offering can be trained or there are lots of people available with the talents you need in employees (for example, social media skills, sales associates, hosts).

- The cost of production goes down with volume.

- The cost of selling goes down with volume.

- The customer experience does not go down with volume.

- Distribution capacity is high and flexible.

- Customer acquisition methods are well known and replicable without needing to depend on a small number of individuals (like the founder to do the selling).

- Customer support and returns processing needs are minimal or automated.

- The selling cycle is generally short.

- Demand is high or could be high with the right offering.
- Customers buy more than one time typically.
- Key supplies are not limited.
- And the most important element—the culture—is the cultural footprint being set correctly— and are you and your early employees modeling the values you desire to build?

Think like Thomas Edison when thinking about scale. He was not successful *only* because he persevered through thousands of materials in search of one that met the specs of a bulb's filament. Edison was successful because he was systematic in his thinking. A single bulb might be fine to light up a parlor, but he desired to light up a city, so he designed a system to accomplish that goal—the electrical grid we love, and ignore today, except when it's not working.

Design for total demand, changes in demand, and where and when that demand may be coming from when designing your manufacturing, service, or creative production delivery.

Go Forth and Replicate

"How to Scale a Business." That has echoes of the Academy Award–nominated *How to Train Your Dragon* by DreamWorks. Is that title a challenge by the way, or is it more of a dare? Someone must know how to train a dragon since that person lived to tell a story about it. So it can be done. If a dragon can be trained, surely a business can be scaled.

If you've been alert during dragon class, you'll know there is a way to develop a creative business idea, from a tiny SPARK through the childhood and adolescent years of CLICK, all the way to the launch and eventual scaling of GO.

If you've shaped your idea, built and tested prototypes and a smart manufacturing approach, designed useful ways to attract and retain customers, and automated some of this—if not all of this—you can scale a business. To scale a business, the basics need to be sound.

And that is what you are doing when you decide which elements of your business to automate and which not to.

Again, you ask: "How do you train a dragon?"

"Very carefully," I say.

Often—and foolishly—overlooked is the need to ensure the culture is correct before scaling. If the recipe is bad as a single batch, do you think making it in army-mess-hall portions is going to make it better—or even the same?

The definition I like to use for culture in my workshops with clients is the operationalization of values.

Culture is like DNA. If the code, when nurtured, results in a strong and agile entity suited to the time and place, then perfect, go forth and replicate. If not, don't. If you do not have a strong nucleus to your culture, scaling will be a nightmare.

The experience we have at Starbucks is similar wherever we go in the world. That's not an accident. Starbucks hiring, training, and everyday management practices reinforce the company's core values and strengthen its culture. When the company fails to live up to its own standards, it digs in and tries again to get it right, falling short, but working to live by its own values, as has happened with the company's handling of racial inequities.

The culture of Starbucks is about making everyone feel comfortable in this third place between home and work, and that can only be achieved if employees are treated as human beings with dignity and respect. It can only happen if employees know they are expected to live—to embody—the company's values every time they put on that apron.

Having the right culture in place is essential to scaling.

The SPARK-CLICK-GO Journey is about gearing up and taking the right steps so you can go as far as you like. Not all entrepreneurs want to create a massive business or one that becomes a household name. The journey is about bringing your creative business idea to life and returning a level of profits and enjoyment appropriate for you.

Automating can make you leaner, more agile, and ready to scale. Automating and building the ability to scale into the fabric of your enterprise will raise the value for you, your customers, and anyone else who may become interested, like employees and investors.

Reflect & Act

- Where do you want to be on the automation continuum—Stone Age or Silicon Age, or somewhere in between?

- The elements of your creative business idea that reflect your personality should be considered core areas—places where you do not want to automate. Be clear in which areas you might deploy automation, and in which areas you will not.

- Are you thinking about scalability and your growth desires as you build your processes? Have you thought about your values and getting the DNA right for your culture?

14
Gettin' Better All the Time

Here's the scene: A conference room with no windows somewhere north of Denver. It's midmorning on day three of a highly intense workshop on strategy, innovation, and execution. About two dozen high-potential leaders from a successful health/industrial tech company are present and engaged. The topic for the session I am leading is innovation.

We look into something called the Table of Disruptive Technologies put out by the Tech Foresight group (www.imperialtechforesight.com) and the Imperial College of London, which categorizes coming innovations such as self-writing software, diagnostic toilets, and buildings that digest pollution on factors like impact on society and how soon they will become available.

But these new technologies do not get my group excited, nor does the idea of disruptive technologies in general. What gets them excited is talking about how they work every day to improve the products and services they offer their current customers.

When I ask participants where they spend their energy with respect to innovation, the answer is continuous improvement, things like defeaturing a product or improving workflows for customers, rather than on coming up with completely new products and services for existing or future customers.

Kaizen, a Japanese word meaning "improve for the better," had become an essential part of this company, and if you took share value as a measure, it was working. Involving and empowering a broad array of employees, understanding customers by going to them, and being transparent about performance in a visual way were some of this company's methods for improving their business. And by not always focusing on the latest shiny object, the company avoids some of the tumult that arises with more major innovation.

On the way to creating the KO Fire Curtain, Tom Oswald, the product's inventor and founder of a company by the same name, himself a former New York City firefighter, told me how important it was for firefighters to get together immediately after battling a significant fire, or one that was unusual, or a fire where lives were lost or people were harmed. They did this to debrief, to discuss what went wrong, what went right, and how as a team they could improve for a similar situation next time. If the FDNY debriefs after events to get better, maybe you can too.

Speaking of New York City, the city used a process called Compstat to clean up the city in the 1990s. Each week, the police department went through debriefs of crime stats on each precinct to pinpoint hot spots and patterns and to figure out how to allocate resources to solve the problem. Individual precinct leaders were held accountable for addressing crime surges in their precincts, and everyone involved committed to a shared set of crime reduction goals.

According to NBC these weekly data-driven social huddles, when leaders had to stand up in the spotlight, were part of a plan that resulted in a 75 percent drop in crime in the city.

Software start-ups do debriefs weekly with a meeting where each team member talks about what they worked on that week, what went well, where they were having challenges, and maybe where they felt they might need help.

Debriefs like these bring accountability out into the open, creating social pressure to perform, while bringing group problem-solving to the fore.

Watch, Listen, and Double-Down

Here's another way to improve your business. Let's say you've worked on building your business using the SPARK-CLICK-GO methodology and your service offering, and how you are doing business is still not hitting the mark. What do you do?

One approach is to double-down on anything that is working. This should be called the Amazon strategy, because that is what Amazon, and its battalions of logistic and seller bots, does—it doubles down on what's working.

If you notice something unexpectedly creating demand that might seem like a distraction, stop what you are doing and investigate—your spidey senses may be tingling for a reason.

Hayde López Rodríguez doubled down when she noticed that people staying at her guest house in Guanajuato, Mexico, most of whom were students at the local university, were in need of better Spanish skills and enjoyed practicing Spanish with her. Out of this initial SPARK, Rodríguez developed teaching skills in herself and others and created Escuela Mexicana, an internationally recognized immersion Spanish language school that has been spreading her love of Mexican culture and the Spanish language for twenty years now.

I learned this lesson about listening to your customers the hard way when I was heading up the cardiovascular therapy area in Canada for a European pharmaceutical company. We had priorities in terms of products on the market, products in early stages of development, and those we were preparing to launch. And so it came as a surprise when I suddenly heard from doctors that they wanted to use an old drug in a new way.

Using a drug previously disallowed for heart failure to now treat heart failure seemed crazy to me from a therapeutic, regulatory, and reimbursement perspective. What had previously been anathema was now avant-garde scientifically. The signal blared on so I had a team look into the feasibility of bringing a version of the drug to market. Even though some doctors were seeking the old drug for this new purpose, we decided the barriers were just too big, and the reward too small. The juice was not worth the squeeze.

I think about this experience even now because I realize that a group of customers demanding that I jump through some hoops to deliver something of value to them is a group of people too important to ignore, even if the distraction was of lower value than planned projects. I don't know how big that business may have become had we pursued it. The outcome is in the land of counterfactuals.

I allowed myself to downplay the problem these key customers were trying to solve and in so doing downplayed how these doctors may have become advocates and allies if given the chance to jump into the trenches and fight for the solution they wanted for their patients. I did not double-down when demand showed itself from an unexpected place. Don't make the same mistake I did. Investigate, then act.

Easy Sells

If your business is working well and you had a strong launch, here's something for you to now think about. If you did not have the chance to think about the metrics you would use to monitor your business as you worked through SPARK-CLICK-GO, now is the time to do so. Pick an area like manufacturing quality, return rates, or repeat purchases from customers and make that part of how you will improve your business. Ask yourself what your goal is in each area in which you choose to measure.

According to an article by Ashley Verrill at *Software Advice*, "A Zappos Lesson in Customer Service Metrics," the highly successful online shoe retailer measures the amount of time customer loyalty team members spend talking with customers, rather than how many customers they talk with. And the company tracks to see if agents tried at least twice to make a personal emotional connection with any given caller. (I guess this is why many of us are asked, "So, hey, how's your day going" or "What have you got going on for the weekend" more and more.) The point is that the metric you choose is a reflection of what you value, what you want more of in your business.

If your creative business idea is about one main product or service, then focus your efforts on improving that one product or service. If your creative business idea is about delivering lots of products or services, then focus on broadening the scope of your offerings, tailoring them better to your audience, or reducing friction in your business for all involved.

Reducing friction is a constant battle for any business—yet it is well worth doing—and it's a critical way to improve your business. If you manage to deliver your offering in one week now, can you figure out how to deliver in five days? If it takes a new customer ten minutes to buy something from your website, can you reduce that to three minutes? If you know much about physics—I have a minor in physics from my undergraduate days—inertia is the force that keeps objects at rest in place. Remove inertia and friction wherever you see it.

Your job: make it as easy as possible for your suppliers to supply you and for your customers to buy from you.

Are You Improving by Pushing Each Element of Your Creative Business Idea?

Remember now for a moment the definition of a creative business idea and its elements to make your business better. Are you deploying an original or imaginative idea and, if so, have you fully executed on your idea?

In my case, with SPARK-CLICK-GO I wanted to inspire people to go all the way—to go beyond an initial idea, to the shaping and testing of it and ultimately to bringing their creative business idea to life. To do this I would provide the concept, the inspiration, and the tools to do so.

With this book my aim has been to highlight the concept and give you, the reader, inspiration to pursue your own idea. I have hinted at the tools. To fully deliver on my original idea, I will need to go beyond where the book leaves off to develop more tools and make them available, and maybe on to the creation and release of other form factors like video to share with, and inspire, people.

Twitter was originally an idea Jack Dorsey and cofounders Noah Glass, Biz Stone, and Evan Williams (and a developer named Florian Webber) created according to a *Business Insider* article by Nicholas Carlson, April 2011. The original idea, largely attributed to Dorsey, was to create an SMS-based method "that revolved around status—what people were doing at a given time."

The service was first used by the nerd class, became popular at a SXSW conference in the spring of 2007, then became big for celebrities to share what they had for breakfast with fans before its purpose shifted to being a news app for what's happening now. The Twitter heads are constantly asking themselves how they can better deploy original or imaginative ideas to make Twitter more accountable and better at delivering on its promise of being about what's happening now.

Does your business reflect who you uniquely are, and could you make it do so even more?

Are you putting enough of yourself into your business? Would people who know you say, without taking a breath, that your business is really you? Are you allowing yourself to be open, maybe even a bit vulnerable when you think about the depth of how the business is, or is not, a true reflection of who you are?

Manolo López found a way to marry his love of cooking and his homeland, Puerto Rico, with business. When hurricane Maria struck Puerto Rico in 2017, López became worried for his family and friends, and for the people of the island, his people. He found a way to visit his homeland and quickly raised money in New York to feed people made desperate by the worst storm in a hundred years.

In the wake of Maria, according to the *Duolingo* podcast, "[López] decided he would become an international spokesman for Puerto Rican culture and cuisine. His new business would combine his cooking with talks about Puerto Rico." That would allow him to put his cuisine—especially mofongo, a dish centered around fried green plantains and the namesake for his business—in its cultural context as an ambassador.

Today Manolo López gives talks about his beloved homeland as he introduces Puerto Rican cuisine around the world and brings the comfort of home to the diaspora wherever they live.

Value Is in the Eye of the Beholder

Does your business bring value to your customers? How do you know? Do you know what in particular your customers, especially your core customers, value about your business and how you can continue to bring value? If you can understand how your customers define value, then you can figure out how to deliver more of it to them and, in so doing, improve your business.

For me, and my mission to help people bring their creative business ideas to life, I hope to hear from readers like you with tales of how you brought a creative business idea from SPARK all the way to GO. That would confirm to me that my efforts brought value to my audience.

While spontaneous feedback will be useful, I could proactively survey readers to learn more about what they valued most in the book and how reading it may have spurred them to action.

Here are two of the best signals proving your customers are deriving value from your business:

- Repeat usage of your product or service
- Unsolicited recommendations or referrals to your business

Achieving both is like finding the Holy Grail.

During the COVID-19 crisis when video conferencing became mainstream, one service really took off, Zoom. Have you asked yourself why that was the case when many other similar services from BlueJean to GoToMeeting to Microsoft Teams and Google Hangouts Meet were available?

Once I tried Zoom, I realized it was easy to use, that the sound was in sync—this was not an overdubbed foreign language soap opera—and the camera options for viewing your friends were varied and easy to change so much so that I felt like a newsroom producer. I noticed as well that I could scale up or down easily with the system—having three or thirty others in the picture just worked well. I wanted to and did use it again and then again.

Zoom got repeat business, and as customers like me used it more, the more we naturally invited others to a Zoom meeting, and naturally we shared our enthusiasm for the experience. Viral growth ensued out of this virtual cycle. Notice the core reason was ease of use in a variety of situations and a seamless experience.

Here's a way to challenge yourself and think about bringing more value to your customers.

A formula for value that I credit to Professor Mark Vandenbosch from my days as a student of Western Ontario's Ivey School of Business can be useful here: Value = Utility / Cost. Value is always viewed from the perspective of the person being served.

With this simple, yet powerful equation in mind, what can you do to bring more value to the person being served by your business? Two types of answers work in this thought experiment. Either you

- Raise utility, or
- Lower cost

Multiple ways are open to you and your team to raise utility, just as there may be more than one path to reducing cost for the person you are serving. You could, of course, do both.

So brainstorm ways to raise utility and lower cost. Figure out, ideally with the involvement of your core customers, what they value and what the costs are for them to use your product or service and, as with all things SPARK-CLICK-GO, get creative.

Uber delivered more value by providing an app to call for a ride, cashless payment, and tipping (eventually) through the app, detailed receipts, ability to rate and know a bit about your driver, nicer cars (theoretically) while lowering costs compared to taxi rides.

You can find ways to make your business a better reflection of who you are. You can increase the value customers get from your product or service. You can do a better job of deploying original or imaginative ideas to make your business better. Like Disney, you can keep the magic flowing.

Reflect & Act

- If you have the outcomes you desired because of SPARK-CLICK-GO, keep improving them. If not, go back to one of the elements in the journey and start again from there. If your prototype did not cut it during the CLICK phase in an important area like performance to an outside standard, or if your customer acquisition model was too costly to ever help you become profitable, go back.

- If you did not have a chance to automate or otherwise make efficient a particular business process, like customer onboarding, do so now.

- Have you decided which metrics are essential for you to monitor in order to maintain and improve your business? Have you asked your customers how they derive value from your offering and, if so, is the value equation working? If not, figure out what you need to do to raise utility or lower costs for your customers.

15
Fuel Your Venture

My dad, being of Irish and Scottish descent, would often say, "If you have two problems and one of them is money, you have only one problem." While not literally true, money *is* really important, but you don't need an accounting degree to figure out the basics.

For example: How much money do you need?

"Funding takes a minimum of six months per round so my rule of thumb," said Adam Lorant, angel investor, entrepreneur, and recipient of a Top 40 Under 40 award in Canada, "is to raise enough money for eighteen months. Twelve months to execute, then six months before raising for the next round."

Depending on the field of business you are operating in, you may need more than this. In the med-tech field, a group of mentors I work with suggested to the company CEO we were mentoring that a minimum of two years' worth of funding should be raised when first bringing a product to market, and that conservative assumptions about revenue build and time to profitability is prudent.

Another way to think about it: Shoot to secure enough money to get you through the phase you are in, including a major milestone, plus an ample cushion.

The cushion is needed to account for things that are late, or for things that never become solid, for the human tendency to make horrible estimates, and for what used to be called acts of God, and now are called *force majeure*. As in, "Vengeance to *force majeure* alone belongs." For severe, and unexpected disruptions, like COVID-19.

The good news: You may not need a lot of cash to explore needs and develop your concept or to figure out if your business idea CLICKs with intended—or unintended—users. Here's what the relative amount of cash needs might be through the stages of SPARK-CLICK-GO:

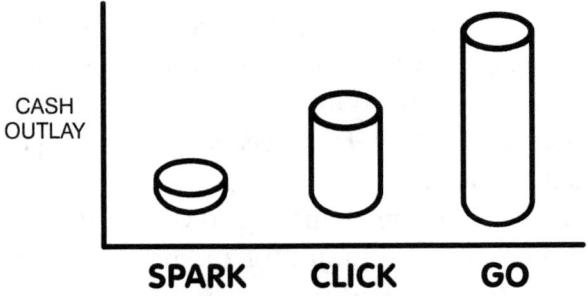

START WITH WHATEVER MONEY AND RESOURCES YOU HAVE AVAILABLE.

If you are in the SPARK phase, you *may* not need, strike that, you *should* not need a lot of money. After all, the SPARK phase is about need exploration and concept development. You don't need a lot of cash to start shaping your idea on paper or as a 3-D model.

This is the bootstrapping or self-funding stage of funding.

In the CLICK phase, you will need enough money to build an early version of your concept, to test and improve it, to get ready to build it, and money to develop branding. This is the seed stage of funding. This is where you are tapping friends and family and angel investors for cash, as a loan or for a piece of equity in the company.

Once you get to the point of building your first release in the GO phase, you may need a chunk of cash, but by then you will have built and learned so much, you will be confident in your idea—and so too will be your investors.

This is typically where you would raise a series A round with more sophisticated investors.

Witness the interest level of the sharks on *Shark Tank*. Watch their enthusiasm rise when a pitching company shows that their product or service is CLICKing with customers, if they've inked a distribution deal, or have a proven, smart business model operating. The sharks don't get into competitive bids over just ideas—they salivate over progress in the marketplace.

And the marketplace—the customer—is where you want to focus.

As Adam Lorant, who has helped generate over a billion dollars of value for investors in the enterprise software space, said to me, "When I put my investor's hat on, I'm looking at reduction of risks."

So if you find yourself enviously thinking or saying stuff like this, take a step back: "Giant Cyprus Capital funded those guys, and those guys are now huge, so therefore (by some leap of logic you don't know how to express) I want them to fund me. And if Giant Cyprus does not fund me, then I must be a loser. My idea must not be any good."

The reason you are not getting funding may have just as much to do with the fact you have not done a stellar job getting your offering right in the SPARK phase, and not getting it to CLICK with the essential audiences.

Fill Your Tank with the Right Kind of Fuel

I'm a simple farm boy from Alberta. Let me rephrase that. I'm a boy from Alberta who knows little about farming. Agro cred aside, my family had a cabin at Pine Lake, Alberta, surrounded by rolling hills and farmers' fields that I frequented during my teenage years and into my twenties with my family, and sometimes just with friends. Thank you, Mom and Dad.

At our cabin, we had a fuel tank like the kind many farmers kept on their properties—the kind that was suspended above the ground on wooden legs like stilts so that gravity was all that was needed to shoot the fuel down the hose and into whatever it was that needed filling—in my case, mostly tanks for our ski boat.

A big tanker would come to all the farms in the area to fill their fuel tanks with cheap diesel. The fuel would last all season. It must have seemed to the farmers like free fuel once it was full. How big the tank needed to be depended on how many vehicles and canisters were being filled, and how often.

So, too, with funding your business. Make sure you have a big enough fuel tank, fill it up, use it judiciously, then get back to farming.

There are two broad types of funding, and only two, available to fuel your venture: dilutive, meaning you are giving up a portion of your enterprise, and nondilutive, meaning you are not.

In both cases you give something up: either some of your future cash goes to paying off debt, or you give up a portion of your company to your investors.

Any money coming into your business, but to a lesser degree with grants and donations, creates an obligation upon you. For every force, there is an equal, and opposite, force. You get the money, but you give something up. See, there's that physics background kicking in again.

Avoiding obligations is one of the reasons cash from sales—profits—is such a pure luxury. If you can be satisfied with that achievement—which is fantastic—and the level of money coming in, super, because that will save you a lot of time spent fund-raising. Time that can be spent instead on meeting customers, developing new or better offerings, and building your business.

With a loan, you will have repayment terms. Should your business be liquidated in the future, your creditor will be standing in line for the money. Should your business progress as expected, paying the loan will be a drag on cash. With an equity investment, someone is taking a portion of your business—and therefore they are entitled to a share of any profit paid out— and, depending on how much equity is owned by others and by you, you may lose control of your venture. With a convertible loan, you have elements of equity and elements of a loan depending on options triggered by your investor or prespecified events.

The chart shows your basic options for fueling your business. Of course, there are many variants and sources, just like with anything else. We are lucky to be living in the age of choice.

	DILUTIVE	NONDILUTIVE
PAY BACK	Convertible Loans	Loans
DO NOT PAY BACK	Equity	Grants, Donations, Out-Licensing Fees, Franchise Fees

BIG SLICE, SMALL PIE? SMALL SLICE, BIG PIE?

Money doesn't grow on trees, but you may find funding sources here:

- Bootstrapping—EQUITY (Founders shares assuming you have incorporated) or DONATION

- Beneficiary—Patreon is one example—DONATION
- Crowdsourcing—Kickstarter is a DONATION
- Grants—DONATION or Subsidy
- Banks—LOAN
- Friends and family—EQUITY or DONATION or LOAN
- Angel investment—EQUITY or LOAN or elements of both (for example, convertible debt—debt that can be converted to equity at a preferential rate)
- Venture capital—EQUITY sometimes LOANS (usually short-term bridging to the next financing round)

My dad also said, "Banks only lend money to people who don't need it." If you have a fantastic business, and especially if you are willing to secure it with, for example, a personal asset like your house (No! Don't do it.), banks will lend you money. Many start-ups lack assets and steady sales needed to get a loan.

The moral of this story? Build a great product, service, or production and you'll be able to dictate your terms and do business with people of your choosing.

Every person setting out to create a business will face a dilemma about funding, except the trustafarians, the trust-fund kids, they're a special breed to themselves who neither need to ask for money nor account for the stuff.

Money does strange things to the rest of us. Pursuing funding takes up a lot of energy, and securing it can bring tensions over three essential elements to the soul of your enterprise:

- Destiny
- Autonomy
- Control

These elements are like food, water, and shelter to your business. Elements you will find yourself fighting for depending on the funding you pursue and the investors you bring into your business.

As Gary Bartholomew, serial tech entrepreneur, put it, typical venture capitalists have "one hand on the money bag, and one hand on the plug."

With any outside financing, but especially with equity financing, you will find yourself fighting a three-headed beast for the soul of your business—you'll be like Hercules fighting Cerberus at the gates of hell. This is a constant battle for aspiring entrepreneurs, at least it can be when growth is concerned. If you are not strong, the three-headed beast will devour you.

The first beast, Destiny, wants to direct your company toward a particular destiny—maybe to pursue a different market or by pushing you to become a premium player when your vision is to serve the masses. Destiny wants to meddle with where you originally wanted to go with your company, or with your reason for being, your mission.

The second beast, Autonomy, wants a bigger say in how you operate the company. Autonomy wants to be involved in more decisions—to micromanage you—your investors are meddling in your affairs, or at least that is how it feels to you.

The third beast, Control, wants more equity or a majority stake in your business as well as seats on your board and certain rights in the governance of your company. They will tempt you with more money, or may help you raise more money, but it is in exchange for more equity being owned by them and not you and your founders. This beast may argue that ceding control is necessary to get more funding, and funding is necessary for scale and growth. Your control be damned.

The key argument Control wields goes something like this: "Wouldn't you rather have a small piece of a big pie than a big piece of a small pie?"

It's a dilemma many entrepreneurs struggle with. In your SPARK-CLICK-GO Journey think through and decide what works for your personality and which approach best fits with the mission of your creative business idea.

Many choose to have a small piece of a big (potential) pie because they want to see their idea grow to be the most it can be, and funding helps them get there.

That small piece of a big pie could become HUGE. It might even win a contest. But will it still hold the sweetness you once enjoyed, and will it look like the kind of pie you set out to bake?

My point: Once you bring in money and interested parties from the outside, you no longer act in a single-minded way to build your company the way you wanted to. That's not always a bad thing, for example, if you find like-minded investors who add a ton of value to your cause over and above the money.

But beware. Many forms of money can impact your destiny, wrest control from you, or force you to manage your business in a way that is not in keeping with your preferences—or worse—your values. Figure out which of these beasts, if any, you are willing to allow in on the show: Autonomy, Destiny, or Control. Then choose your source of funding accordingly.

CHOOSE YOUR INVESTORS WISELY AND BE WARY.

An alternative to equity financing is crowdfunding.

I've had some experience with crowdfunding, in the context of a Startup Weekend event I ran along with the director of an incubator in California where we had teams create a campaign for crowdfunding. The two platforms I am familiar with are Kickstarter and Indiegogo.

In case you are not aware of how these work, you put together a campaign on a platform of choice that describes your product and vision, how much you're trying to raise, and what the rewards are you are offering as an inducement, and then—and this is elemental—you promote the heck out of it using your social media presence, direct emails to contacts, joint promotions, and everything else. A reward is something that people who support your fund-raising campaign over a threshold donation level receive once the product has been developed and is available.

One advantage of crowdfunding is that it is nondilutive, meaning you do not need to give up a portion of the ownership in your business. If you have a successful campaign, you have a built-in group of fans ready to receive your product and tell the world all about it.

You can also crowdfund for equity investments now because of the JOBS act—that could be an option to consider as well. For that you will need to create a profile on Gust or AngelList.

Self-funding is what Alejandro Mendez did with four business partners when starting out what has become Four Monkeys coffee roasting—one of the first roasters in El Salvador. As Alejandro said on the *Duolingo* Spanish podcast (July 15, 2020), the partners pooled their money and bought one sack of coffee and roasted it. With the proceeds they bought two sacks and roasted those. Then three, then four and on from there.

Earnings from sales are a great way to fund your venture because they simultaneously verify that you are providing value to your customer and that your business model is working. Meanwhile, you are maintaining control of your company. You are also taking risks off the table—you won't find yourself stuck with an impatient investor or with high debt repayments should your business hit a slowdown.

The major knock on financing growth out of profits is this: you won't be able to grow your business fast without capital coming in.

Of course, you will need to incorporate your company if you want to raise funds. There are many resources out there to help you. Know that a common choice is to create a C Corp in the state of Delaware if you are doing business in the US. For many simple entities, an LLC will be an appropriate form, or an S Corp. Get your lawyer and your financial guru involved, if you have one.

The modern corporation is a marvelous invention. Legally a corporation is its own entity through which you can

- Create shares,

- Raise money from distributing those shares, and

- Protect yourself from legal liability.

That doesn't mean you have to buy into them as persons, with rights like free speech, as *Citizens United* suggests.

These are many of the reasons to incorporate. So if you are serious about your venture, look into incorporating.

When you incorporate a company and create shares, you can then apportion those shares to founders, early investors, and later-stage investors alike. Shares become a new currency—like Monopoly money—with which you will be able to divvy up the company among its founders and early employees. The shares become a currency that people will accept in lieu of, or to complement, cash. Early shareholders willing to hold shares instead of cash are looking for a long-term payout—they're the kids who can resist one marshmallow now for the promise of two marshmallows later.

As Yuval Noah Harari makes clear in his excellent book *Sapiens*, corporations are social constructs that hold up as long as we all continue granting them legal status as entities through which the funding, discovery, development, manufacturing, and distribution of goods, services, and productions can be facilitated—without exposing individuals to liability.

Creating a corporation can be of immense value to you as a creative business founder. A company is a legal vessel for your venture that you control and through which you can protect yourself from legal liability.

Reflect & Act

- Cash is the lifeblood of all businesses. In the exploratory or SPARK phase, you may want to self-fund your idea. As you move forward to building an early version of your idea, friends and family members or angel investors, as well as granting organizations, and in some cases online crowdfunding can be good sources of cash. When you get to GO, you'll need more cash, which can come from wealthy individuals, investment groups or firms, or institutions in the form of equity and/or debt.

- Every form of money creates an obligation on you and your business with the notable exception of funding that comes from the profits on sales and to some extent grants. Some money forms are dilutive, meaning you are sharing the ownership of the company in exchange for that funding, and some, like debt, are not. Before you face the dilemma, think through whether you want to have a big piece of something small, or a smaller piece of something big.

- Do you have someone on your team or someone you trust to help you create a funding plan and execute it? Or do you have a clear idea of what type of funding makes sense for you now, and for your growth plans, and are you making relationships with those who can help you find it, or are you working directly with investors?

16
Stop Thinking about [BIG] Venture Capital

I mean it. Stop thinking about venture capital.

Most new businesses are not right for venture capital—from the [BIG] VCs in particular.

If your business idea has at least a shot at bringing in multiple hundreds of millions of dollars in sales or more in its first ten years, and your business has the possibility of returning ten dollars for every dollar a [BIG] VC invests, your business might be the exception.

But everyone else, stop thinking about [BIG] venture capital.

Stop thinking about venture capital unless you've already created a solution to a clear and pressing problem that is CLICKing with customers, key opinion leaders, and lab/tech people proving it works. And when that happens, go after the right VC with a fund sized and suited to the field in which your business is operating.

If you are at the seed or early stage, you may do best to go after smaller VCs or angel investors. In theory, angels will fund strong creative business ideas if they believe in the problem being solved and will help entrepreneurs fund the building and testing of early prototypes. Smaller VCs will likely fund businesses only after proof of concept and a product that CLICKs with customers.

But even angel investors have shifted. Many now operate in angel groups and these groups are wanting more due diligence and proof your idea works and that customers are interested before funding an idea.

Everyone wants risk reduction. Which is exactly what SPARK-CLICK-GO is meant to help you with.

So, yes, get to know a few investors in your field and let them know what you're doing, then focus on product, customers, telling your story, customer acquisition, and how you're going to build out your creative business idea.

In general, the bigger the VC (firm and fund), the later the stage of the company they invest in, and the bigger the deals.

According to FundersClub, the average VC deal in 2019 was around $10M for late-stage companies. In 2015, ~$60B was invested by VCs in ~4,500 start-ups, an average of ~$13M per company. Contrast that with ~$25B invested by angel investors in 2015 in ~70,000 start-ups, for an average deal just under $350k.

Venture capital can help businesses that have nailed the problem solution challenge and have traction with customers. VCs can help with a business model, with scaling, or to open doors to partnerships and can add extra capital to businesses that are performing.

Get to know some in your area if you think you may have something of interest to them—this chapter will help you decide—but don't obsess over them. Obsess over your product, your customers, and figuring out how to acquire new customers and how to distribute to them.

As Sergey Babichenko, scientist and entrepreneur, might say, the most important thing once you have investors in place is to show them progress and that you are moving as fast as you can.

Picture this scene playing out in the main hallway of Giant Cypress Capital, Palo Alto, California, where Justin, an associate and recent grad from Stanford business school, bumps into Danielle, a senior partner.

Danielle: "Justin, can we touch base re companies you've been looking at for the new fund?"

Justin: "Umm sure. Well, I've got three possible companies. One is a new streaming service, one is a dating app for older folks, and one is a new diagnostic test based on web searches."

Danielle: "Okay. Tell me what you like about each one."

Justin: "Right. The new streaming service team is entering a huge and growing market, they're small now but their angle is providing content no one else is focusing on, and they're securing licensing deals as we speak."

Danielle: "I see. What about distribution? Any of the big players agree to put them on their platform?"

Justin: "Yah, Amazon has. Google has. They're working on Apple."

Danielle: "Got it. Next."

Justin: "Ah, um. Okay. The dating-app-for-older-folks company has great traction. They're basically OkCupid for the older set, a space no one has really mastered, so the play is tapping into pent-up demand."

Danielle: "Got it. Is the user growth and business model panning out? I mean can you see this thing turning hundreds of millions in revenue in the next five to six years or so?"

Justin: "For sure. Seems like older folks got a lot o' game in 'em still. The key is getting them to use smartphones or their iPads to swipe for a date. The amazing thing is these guys are showing it can be done—they're opening a new vertical and, if successful, they could get a lock on it."

Danielle: "I'd like to see the data. You really need an angle in that space that breaks through yet is big enough to create a network effect. There are so many dating apps out there—a new team seems to walk in the door here every week with a dating app claiming to be the next big thing. So, quickly, give me the topline on your third prospect."

Justin: "The last one is a big-data, machine-learning digital health play. These MIT guys are using people's search data to figure out what kinds of illnesses they might have, and then flagging the insight with the insurance companies. It's kind of a big brother approach to early diagnosis and treatment."

Danielle: "Sounds like HIPAA concerns are going to be key. I like that this is algorithm-based so they may not need heavy clinical testing to get past the FDA. Have they got contracts with any of the big insurance players like Aetna or Blue Cross?"

Justin: "That's right. In fact, they've got a pilot going with Aetna now and they're working with some big regional players in Massachusetts too."

Danielle: "All right. So where are you netting out on this, Justin? We want to take action soon on the best of the bunch that everyone has been seeing so we can build out and eventually close the new fund."

Justin: "Understood. The tough thing is figuring out which one has the best chance of breaking out. I mean, should we try to figure out which one has the best chance of becoming a unicorn ($1B in sales), or do we bet on all three?"

Danielle: "Maybe I can help you narrow it down and figure out if there's a knock-out punch with one or more of them. Are there any where the founders have not had successful exits?"

Justin: "No. They've all had successful exits, two IPOs and one sale to a strategic."

Danielle: "What about the talent mix and level. Do they have the right talent? What's the pedigree, Justin?"

Justin: "The talent is excellent. I think two of the teams have a visionary leader with great tech and business savvy. The web diagnostic team is a bit lighter on that but has fantastic game-changing tech."

Danielle: "I see. What's the tech like for the other two—how novel is it?"

Justin: "I wouldn't say game changing, but the traction is excellent in each case."

Danielle, eyebrows furrowed, voice slightly on edge: "So, what are you going to do, Justin? For God's sake. Are you telling me they are equally likely to be ten baggers?"

Justin: "I think so, I think they should all be in the fund."

Danielle: "Fine but we're not putting extra money in—if we do all three, you're going to have to spread your money around. Maybe you should think about that and figure out what you need to know from each to see if you really want to keep all three. Have them back here for a second pitch and bring me in. I wanna get a feel for them myself before we put any of these guys into due diligence and shoot them out a term sheet."

Justin: "Great. Thanks."

Imagine your company being discussed behind closed doors with VCs. Would snippets of conversation around a water cooler capture your business, the opportunity you're pursuing, your team, and your path to victory with excitement and FOMO (fear of missing out)? That's your goal.

Venture capital is mainly focused in tech, biotech, and clean tech. Leslie Feinzaig, founder and CEO of the Female Founders Alliance, does not think venture capital is right for every business. In a *Fast Company* article, Feinzaig points to these four reasons for VC rejection:

- Something is wrong with the business.
- Venture capital is not the right kind of capital.
- The [pitch and pitchers] failed to persuade them.
- They don't think the team is up for the job.

For many businesses, a loan, partner investment, or grant are acceptable options, said Feinzaig. "Better yet, you might go after the single most valuable type of early start-up capital: real revenue from real customers. Trust me. It rocks."

For the mold breakers—the ones with the grit required of entrepreneurs, the ones willing to pick up a hammer and start nailing in the wake of a hurricane, Skip Klintworth, serial entrepreneur, investor, and entertainment producer, stressed the need to meet increasingly tough tests in order to attract higher levels of funding. "Every stage requires a different proof of concept. The angel investor is going to want to see more than friends and family, and the venture or private equity investor will want to see a whole lot more. Show me a technology that works and a thousand loyal users and we'll talk—maybe."

In his book about venture investing called *Secrets of Sand Hill Road*, Scott Kupor, managing partner at Andreessen Horowitz (a marquee VC firm in Silicon Valley), makes clear how VCs work, what kinds of investments they are looking for, how they get involved with companies including board seat privileges they seek, and the myriad ways in which they ensure they get preferential rights on profits earned.

A few elements stuck with me from Kupor's writing.

Because venture capital firms have limited partners who need to have above-average returns with the small proportion, to them, of capital they invest in the VC fund, and the long holding period, the VC needs to select firms aiming at huge markets, with above-average technology/ solutions, and teams with either a history of building big companies or pedigree (Stanford, Harvard, Yale, MIT, Carnegie Mellon) to offer the potential for a tenfold return on the money invested.

And the big VC firms and funds make big bets—sometimes tens of millions of dollars and above—so your venture needs to have the potential to earn multiple hundreds of millions in revenues with a shot at being the home run that makes the VC model work, to even be considered.

Venture capital firms ensure their interests are looked after through the contracts they sign. They will want a small board, and a seat upon it, so that their voting rights are strong. They will ensure new financing rounds do not dilute their holdings, particularly in what they call down rounds, when your company is valued less than a previous round, and they may want special liquidation rights that pay back their investment if there is a wind-down of the business instead of a public offering (IPO) or acquisition exit.

VCs can be helpful partners, opening many doors, and they can offer a steady investment that can help the right kind of company grow, but they are not for everyone—they are for the select few.

I like Kupor's book and have recommended it to several early-stage CEOs. If you think your company may be VC material, or if you just want to learn more about these mysterious heroes of capitalism—the financiers behind many of the big tech companies with whom we are, by now, intimately familiar, and them with us—pick up a copy.

Here's a test to see if your creative business idea might be of interest to the [BIG] venture capital firms/funds:

Think of three hurdles each with its own rule of tens.

> HURDLE 1:
> Is your team, timing, and traction a ten on a ten-point scale? If so, that might get you in the door.

The next test.

> HURDLE 2:
> Does your business hold the possibility to deliver a tenfold improvement on the current solution and return ten times the VC's investment during a ten-year time horizon?

Fabulous.

HURDLE 3:
Is the trajectory of your revenue or user base 10 x 10 x 10—that is, an exponential path in the ballpark of $10M to $100M to $1B?

Smaller VCs investing fewer dollars in earlier stage companies follow this same pattern, just on a smaller scale.

Reflect & Act

- VCs of all sizes need to hit home runs to make their ROI targets. They can be very helpful in opening doors and bringing additional capital to you if your business is performing. But they're not for everyone or even for most businesses.

- I hope you've gained some insight as to how they think and operate. If you think you might fit the mold, do your homework to target the right firms and try to get an introduction from a company they are already funding or have funded in the past. That's the best way in.

- The smaller VC funds make smaller, earlier stage deals. Do some additional reading and research and talk to people in your field. If this is the way you want to go, do the hard work of developing your product and gaining traction with customers to show them you can be their next grand slam.

17
Got Talent?

This is about having the right people rowing the boat. Or, if you prefer, the right people in your rocket *and* in your control room. It's about starting your venture with the right talent at the core.

Think of the creativity portrayed by the people working in the command center, and by the astronauts, in the movie *Apollo 13*. Stream it when you next get a chance if you haven't seen this gem by Ron Howard—or watch it again. These talented folks show the kind of roll-up-your-sleeves problem-solving skills and can-do attitude all ventures need to survive and thrive.

A creative business idea can start out as a solo operation, or with multiple founders.

Your venture can be a solopreneur-ship—a one woman show—or it can be a bigger venture with you at the helm. Small ventures can start out with one main person rowing the boat, and stay small, or they can grow into big enterprises.

Drybar started out as one person, Alli Webb, driving around LA wielding a blow dryer and styling kit, delivering blowout hairstyling in women's homes, and grew into a salon-based thriving franchise business that has employed more than 3,000 stylists.

One benefit to a single person as the sole or main founder—there is a strong chance of making sure the business is a true reflection of that founder. That's a huge benefit, one that can be made real if the founder can attract and ignite others to their cause whether as paid staff or cohorts who receive shares.

Most businesses I can think of start out with two founders, and certainly with fewer than five founders.

The dynamic duo approach is a time-tested pattern in the creation of businesses. Think: Steve Jobs and Steve Wozniak, Bill Gates and Paul Allen, Larry Page and Sergey Brin.

And there are many duos in music and the arts: Paul Simon and Art Garfunkel, Elton John and Bernie Taupin, Lin-Manuel Miranda and Thomas Kail, Captain and Tennille.

In country building: Washington and Hamilton.

The dynamic duo approach has many benefits:

- Everything is 50/50.

- Voting is not the way decisions are made (as soon as you get to three, voting becomes an option).

- Accountability is high (an analogy: if you have only two roommates living in a house together, you always know who took out the trash—and who didn't).

The triple threat approach can work well too. A famous threesome: Brian Chesky, Joe Gebbia, and Nathan Blecharczyk of Airbnb.

The triple threat approach has some benefits:

- You can cover three areas of business such as product development, operations and marketing, and business development.

- Consensus decision-making can still be accomplished relatively easily, but if you have to vote, a triad works (I suggest you spell out what kinds of matters require the consent of all three founders so that your default method for making decisions does not become voting).

- Diversity of thought is stronger with three parties involved.

The rock group approach is another form to found a venture upon. Rock bands often find their groove with four members. There were four Beatles—each with strong talents and appealing personalities. But before that, there were just two.

John Lennon and Paul McCartney met at a church garden party in Liverpool where Lennon was playing with his band, the Quarrymen. McCartney, according to NPR (citing *The Beatles Anthology* documentary), said he thought Lennon "was making a very good job of it [playing a pretty crappy guitar]."

Lennon was introduced to McCartney's talents that night too—either backstage or during an invitation to join the Quarrymen on stage—and was likewise impressed with McCartney, so he asked him to join the band. That was the SPARK.

It was a great beginning, but it was not enough.

Biography.com, also quoting *The Beatles Anthology* (a documentary in the band members' own words) wrote: "Though still performing as the Quarrymen, Lennon, McCartney and Harrison would go on to form the core that would soon become the Beatles."

Later when Ringo Starr was hired to replace Pete Best, and the band started working with George Martin, they really CLICKed. Martin would go on to produce some of the band's biggest hits.

The rock group approach has some benefits:

- You can cover four or more areas of business.

- You can fit in a single vehicle.

- You can play doubles tennis when you have a chance for a physical break.

The songwriting power was really the duo of Lennon and McCartney, or one of them on their own, with Ringo Starr and George Harrison adding the occasional composition.

Lennon and McCartney were really the founders—Harrison, Starr, and Martin made them a team.

The real questions when forming your venture are these: Are the core talents and traits embedded? Is there a commitment to a shared vision for the business? and Is the chemistry among the founders a catalyst for unbounded creativity and success?

Having irreplaceable talents, traits, and chemistry—these should be your guide.

If you need stellar design and compelling marketing to succeed long term, and if you are the designer, then hook up with a compelling marketer. But don't bring someone in as a founder who brings skills your venture only needs at the start. Remember, you can always hire specific skills that may be needed sporadically.

With whom might you want to found a company?

Adam Lorant, serial tech entrepreneur and investor, suggests entrepreneurs establish their ventures on their own or with one other person with whom they share these traits:

- A strong passion and commitment to the mission they are about to embark on

- Complementary talents and personalities

- A deep and mutual trust, respect, and confidence

If you find your match, fantastic, you should be in good shape. You can always hire as necessary to augment the team you are trying to create.

Bob Gaudio and Frankie Valli were essential to the Four Seasons. Bob wrote the songs; Frankie was the voice. But they needed Bob Crewe to produce the music.

If you have the talent, but not the commitment in one founder, keep looking.

Finding the right talent is exactly what one of the most successful progressive rock bands did—one you may never have heard of—when it was struggling to find its soul. After years of playing around Toronto in small venues, and even covering a Buddy Holly tune—not something you'd expect of a band inspired by Led Zeppelin, Cream, and the Who—Geddy Lee and Alex Lifeson replaced their percussionist with Neil Peart.

Peart was a wizard with the drums and proved to be a lyricist whose artful tastes complemented the musical writing sensibilities and focus on musicianship that Lee and Lifeson embodied.

With Peart on board, a chemistry and shared vision was created that would propel Rush forward into rock history. Early on, the band created their own label and started down a unique path. It was the beginning of their mission to take rock music to a more artistic plain.

The new trio got right to work releasing two all-original albums in the mid-1970s. Peart's elevated lyrics in the song "Rivendell," based on J. R. R. Tolkien's fiction, was a sign of things to come. The band had started to forge a unique identity—one far from the identity of a cover band playing Buddy Holly tunes.

During this creative blossoming, Rush released what the group describes as their magnum opus, *2112*, later recognized as one of the top prog rock albums of all time according to *Rolling Stone* magazine.

Rush had CLICKed internally as the trio of Lifeson, Lee, and Peart, and they were starting to CLICK with audiences. In the studio and on stage, they were soaring.

Among rock bands, only the Beatles and the Rolling Stones have more consecutive gold or platinum albums.

Rush created twenty-four gold records, eleven platinum, and three multi-platinum albums.

The trio of Lifeson, Lee, and Peart created and performed music as Rush for five decades. Neil Peart died in January 2020 of brain cancer. RIP, professor.

Contrast this with the original dream team in basketball made up of some of the most talented players the game has ever seen.

Dream teams might be the jam for short-lived sprints like a global competition every four years, but they are expensive and prone to ego-driven squabbles and, over a longer term, often implode.

I'm usually skeptical when I come across a solo founder—I wonder whether that person will be able to sell their vision to others and get their commitment.

"But a solo founder might be perfectly fine," says Adam Lorant and that, in his experience as a founder and investor, "success hinges on whether that person is capable of recruiting talented people to fill skill gaps, and whether that person can inspire, delegate, and work effectively with the people who form what is essentially his management or executive team."

Three is a good number of founders to start a business with.

Four is getting to be too many.

Two is the ideal number of founders.

But not just any two, or three, or four. Picking the right cofounder(s) is critical and is really tough. Lorant says, "It's like getting married to another person when you don't really know them."

Think of it like this: who would you gather together if you were climbing Kilimanjaro?

When an invite came to me from a friend in 2018 to make the trek to the roof of Africa, a flood of questions arose, among them: What kinds of tasks would need to be done? What risks do we need to plan for? Do we have the skills, commitment, and resilience we need among our group and with our guides?

With any meaningful and challenging journey, there is a goal, there are choices to be made, resources and skills needed, risks and setbacks to be anticipated and planned for, experience to be drawn on, discipline and preparation to train for and execute, and an I've-got-your-back kind of attitude among the team if you are to succeed.

And you will have setbacks. This is but one tough setback our group experienced during our ascent on Kilimanjaro: Mid-expedition, we trekked to 4,600 meters elevation to Lava Tower from where we took in the long views of the valley, took a few photos, and enjoyed a hearty lunch. During the previous four days or so, we had trekked to within 1,300 vertical meters of the summit—our goal seemed close.

From that high perch, our guides led us down, down, down to Moira Hut camp to spend the night, before again heading higher the next day along the northern route. Climb high, sleep low was the tactic our guides were using to keep altitude-sickness from invading our group. It was a prudent approach, but I have to say, I had never seen our group of trekkers, nor felt myself, more dispirited than that night in camp.

The summit, our goal, was farther on this day then it had been twenty-four hours earlier. What could we do? Get up the next day, cheer on each other, and put one foot in front of the other. We had a summit to mount.

So, too, is the journey of bringing a creative business idea to life.

Working with a set of founders on a direct detection diagnostic technology for coronavirus, I experienced something similar to the setback on Kilimanjaro. Our team had worked diligently early on in the pandemic's rage to secure a grant, which would spring-load our technology development toward the point of proof of concept. The request for innovation specs BARDA, the granting body, had written, were a perfect match for what we were aiming to develop and bring to market.

When that grant funding and another grant fell through—two tough setbacks in rapid succession—the team's spirit sank. The founders and team had to dig deep. The founders went on a fund-raising mission, and a few months later, an injection of private capital from a partner that shared the team's vision was negotiated and secured. An injection that would fuel the team's tech to proof of concept, and a relationship with the promise to carry the business well beyond the lab.

In both setbacks, experience mattered as did a mature and unrelenting focus on the goal. In both cases, an adventurer's mindset, and the resourcefulness that comes with it, was key among the leaders and the team members involved.

Setbacks are a given with any start-up, and resiliency within the team is an absolute must.

The better your creative business idea, the better your CLICK with the five essential audiences, the more likely you will be to attract solid people to your cause. Make sure to pick talented people who are excited by your mission and who embody your values.

Reflect & Act

- I write about rock bands because they are visible to us. We have all seen the tensions, the breakups, the heartache, and the resentment that can result when strong egos try to work together. It's a good analog for start-ups. You could also watch the movie *The Social Network* to get an idea of the tension that arises and the kinds of betrayals that take place when battles over the soul of a creative business idea ensue.

- Do you personally or does your founding team share a vision for your business and do you have the talent you need to develop and execute on your creative business idea? Have you, or has your founding team together, overcome significant obstacles in the past and become stronger as a result? Do you, and your team, have the bandwidth and stick-to-itiveness to create and grow this idea into reality?

- To expose whether you have the kind of chemistry and resilience you will need to soar, think of a real-life or tough simulated challenge you and your team can undertake, and go do it. Meet some challenges together before you conquer the world.

18
Bloopers and Blunders

Look. Famous people f*ck up. It's something they do to prove they are human. They are human and therefore they are learning from their mistakes. And purely for our entertainment, they occasionally f*ck up.

The silver lining? You can learn from their pitfalls.

In 1993 Steven Spielberg and Jeffrey Katzenberg entered the themed restaurant business with Dive!, a submarine-themed offering, according to Mental Floss, inspired by Spielberg's fascination with the sea.

> "Inside was a complete stainless-steel aesthetic, with portholes, torpedo-shaped bar seats, and a periscope that could survey the affluent Los Angeles commercial district [of Century City, California]. The climax to this simulated nautical submersion was timed to hit every 45 minutes: For 30 seconds, contained water would cover the portholes, lights would flash, and the groaning sounds of a submerged submarine would be piped in through speakers, giving diners the illusion of being lowered into the depths while gorging on $11.95 gourmet submarine sandwiches, the franchise's signature dish."

Spielberg's name reportedly helped a lot with the launch, but would that be enough to keep this ship sailing?

Sadly, no. The restaurant went under several years later succumbing to a lack of retail sales of merchandise, a key component of themed restaurants according to Mental Floss. A second installment in Las Vegas bottomed out five years into the venture.

Providing a great experience is essential for service businesses. In business you have to connect with enough people on an emotional level if you want them to engage with your offering and your mission. That's why building a business that is a reflection of you counts. Maybe a *Jaws*-themed eatery would have been a truer fit, or maybe entertainment of the recorded variety is the right creative business idea.

For all business ventures there is a product or service on offer that CLICKs with enough people for a long enough period of time, or it doesn't. Learnings abound in these situations.

A blooper, or spontaneous bungle, is a by-product of people making an effort to create something. Bloopers are normally associated with movies or TV shows, but they happen everywhere, including in business.

Sometimes start-up ventures have to just put something out there and keep working to improve that something—a go-to-market version may really be a prototype, something kinda ugly that works just well enough. A little embarrassing? Yes, but, boy, do the teams involved learn a ton in the doing.

Think of Hyundai automobiles in the early twenty-first century, or Japanese cars in the eighties and nineties. Both manufacturers improved on their designs each year eventually leading to vastly improved offerings, strong sales, and loyal buyers.

An Airbnb blooper might be the original photos taken by hosts, complete with unmade beds and messy living rooms lit like dungeons, improved upon massively with professional photographers taking photos of hosts' spaces that have been staged at least a little to look professional. The company's original name could be seen now as a kind of blooper too: AirBedandBreakfast. Not so sexy.

Facebook's blooper was the ratings site first created so that (mostly male) Harvard students could vote on the attractiveness of their female classmates in a sort of twisted, adolescent face-off.

Do you remember the Newton? The Newton was Apple's not-ready-for-prime-time version of a PDA—a personal digital assistant front-runner to the iPhone that really could not do much in the Mesozoic era, way back before Tim Berners-Lee bolted the world wide web to the internet. The Newton was a complete flop commercially—we can laugh about it now—but you and I both know how the story unfolds. Apple is now one of the world's few trillion-dollar companies.

How about the airplane? The Wright brothers nearly died on their quest to take the first manned flight. Had you been there on the dunes of Kitty Hawk, North Carolina, in those early days of the nineteenth century, you might have laughed as the pair of bicycle mechanics from Ohio risked their lives attempting to raise a plane into the air from their sandy, hillock perches. Yet they beat the French to the claim of inventing manned flight and, in the doing, soared into history.

And the Winner Is—

A blunder is a careless or clumsy mistake. I've come up with a few awards for common blunders in bringing a creative business idea to life:

The **SPARK that Does Not CLICK** award goes to the team with the solution that does not fit the market need.

The **Solution Looking for a Problem** award goes to the team who has a solid solution, but the problem is not widespread, and so there's not much of a market to tap. This type of problem sometimes works itself out, and over time people recognize the potential of the solution, or they use it in new ways leading to strong sales.

The **SPARK that Ignites a Market** award goes to the team that comes up with a solution that seems to create a market out of nothing. The ride-sharing solutions seemingly created a massive market out of the ether. Prior to ride-sharing apps, the idea of hailing a stranger's car to get across town was antithetical to most people's idea of a solid idea.

The **Bad News Bears** award goes to the worst team. The award goes to the well-intentioned but hopelessly unorganized team, or to the team without the right skills and experience to execute on the idea—to win the game—right now.

The **Scrooge** award goes to the team that is running so tight financially that time-saving tools and expertise are not brought into the company at the right time.

The **Elizabeth Holmes of Theranos** award goes to the team that does not have working technology but, rather, lots of window dressing in the form of public relations. The tech fails the Lab People's tests. It does not CLICK.

THE THURSTON HOWELL AWARD

The **Thurston Howell III** award goes to the team with too much money given the lack of strength of their technology, their team, their plan, or their business model. Where is a team going to spend all that money on a tropical island with Gilligan and the professor and a few aboriginal tribes and no shops?

The **Gwyneth Paltrow** award goes to the team with the worst business or brand name. Goop? Really? Drybar was almost called Straight Bar, an extension of the name for Alli Webb's mobile business. Note, the modifier, *almost*.

The **All SPARK and No CLICK** award goes to the team with a product that everyone wants to try once. Well at least that's how it was for me living in Canada when Krispy Kreme donuts first rolled into town. Donuts so melt-in-your-mouth delicious these hot numbers were worth the drive across town to try—once. Then back to the old standby, Timmies. This could have been called the Krispy Kreme award.

The **Death of a Salesman** award goes to the team with the most expensive customer acquisition model relative to profit.

The **Land Rover** award goes to the team with a sleek design without the engineering chops to match. Aren't these babies gorgeous—Range Rover, Land Rover, all the rovers are handsome 4x4s, and the pedigree is fantastic. In Africa, these beasts roam the savannah endlessly, but don't try them in the city unless you want, so I am told, to roam the dealer repair shop endlessly.

The **Neil Young** award goes to the entrepreneur who does not evaluate whether their idea CLICKs with the essential five audiences. Young's high-fidelity digital music player PonoPlayer was not appreciated by the masses, and the audiophiles failed to get behind the product. Keep on rockin' in the free world, Mr. Young—we still love you.

The **Do Not Pass GO** award goes to the team that fails to launch big in a field where that just can't be done.

The **Homer Simpson** award goes to the team that does not go all the way with SPARK-CLICK-GO, but instead started numerous ideas but gave up too early without any focused development and testing.

The **Charity Case** award goes to the team that gives it all away free. Alternatively, this award is known as the "Hey, this is not a creative business idea" award.

The **Mr. Wonderful** (Kevin O'Leary of *Shark Tank*) award goes to the team that accepts financing that must be completely paid back *and* gives a portion of the company away to a charming and cunning investor. The funding is both dilutive and a drain on cash.

Bloopers and blunders can be fun and instructive, unless it's you and your company making them. You can learn just as much by taking in what not to do, as you can taking in what to do. Have fun. Don't take yourself too seriously. Smile.

SPARK-CLICK-GO: Mistakes to Avoid

Creative Business Idea

- Noncreative business ideas since that may lead you to a less fulfilling experience or to quitting when the going gets tough

SPARK

- Not shaping your idea early on—not putting the firing of your neurons into form, which may result in inertia and the death of your idea

- Keeping your idea to yourself—failing to share your idea could result in developing the wrong one

- Building an unworthy idea—since that can take all of your time and energy away from a better, more rewarding idea

CLICK

- Going without prototypes—a failure here could be a problem since you may miss the mark with your intended clientele's needs

- Not testing your early and your prerelease versions—failure here and you won't learn—you have to prove the concept and smooth the edges; ultimately, failure here can result in poor uptake

- Not testing branding, packaging, and messaging—can result in less ability to attract people—you may even offend some people inadvertently or your offering may not get noticed

- Putting your head in the sand when it comes to customer acquisition, retention, and revenue models—could result in an unprofitable business and therefore a lack of ability to attract investors

- Not building customer acquisition for your first release and knowing how to provide the right levels of your offering to meet demand—could result in not enough customers and reduced buzz or unsatisfied customers

GO

- Making only a ripple when you need to make a splash—you want standing room only for your launch; "no one goes to a busy restaurant" is your goal

- Expecting your offering to sell itself—failure to sell and support your offering could cause lack of growth or loss of business

- Not automating and scaling your business—failure to automate will curtail efficiency at any size and hamper your ability to scale and grow

Funding and Talent

- The three-headed monster (Destiny, Autonomy, Control), or at least knowing what you are getting into; do not obsess about funding, you should make sure you have enough to get you from SPARK to CLICK to GO or until you are profitable; things to obsess over: your offering, your team, your customers

- Building a creative business without the right talent in place—could result in failure to meet your mission, loss of morale, and relationship and reputational damage

---

Reflect & Act

- People goof up. Even famous actors, politicians, and entrepreneurs. What can you learn from these examples?

- "If you're not falling down, you're not trying hard enough," so said my dad to me about skiing. Bloopers seem funny at the time. The Newton was the name of the first personal digital device envisioned by Apple—it flopped but no one is laughing at Apple now. Are you pushing yourself hard enough, and if not, where should you be pushing your limits?

19
Three Points at the Buzzer

When my family and I lived in New Jersey—New Jersey, that place for me of green pastures, sheep, sunflowers, fireflies, and golden summers—we had the privilege of being parishioners at St. Charles Borromeo Catholic Church in Skillman. St. Charles was then, and is today, headed by an eloquent priest—Monsignor Gregory Malovetz—who is an astounding homilist. I hear Father Greg's voice in my head when I think about his homilies and I write the words *So first*, preceded by something like, "I have three points to talk about today."

I have three points on stuff to get right in bringing your creative business idea to life: Choose an idea worth building. Test, listen, and adapt. Launch when your idea CLICKS, then improve.

So first, choose an idea worth building.

An idea worth building is one where you deploy *imaginative* (I love that word) or original ideas that reflect who you are as a person, while adding value to people's lives and to society. An idea worth building returns a profit sized to your needs, and benefits you, your cofounders, and your investors in financial and in human ways.

Choosing the wrong idea to develop into a business could cost you precious time and your most precious resource, your energy. Choosing something that is not a reflection of you or your passions could rob you of the grit (resiliency) you will need when you, and your team, hit obstacle after obstacle on your way to building something—anything—of value.

One of my creative business ideas is *SPARK-CLICK-GO*. I created it. I think about it often. It has been a long—and rewarding—road from inception to finished product. I have come across many obstacles, any one of which could have stymied me completely. Obstacles like an unexpected move that would again have my wife and me living in a new state. I have had moments of self-doubt—could I really translate my varied business, consulting career, and life experiences into something others might value?

I had nightmares, too, like the one I had in Africa the night before a friend of mine and I were, in real life, to venture to Livingstone Island from the place we were staying on the shoreline of the majestic Zambezi River, above Victoria Falls, Zambia.

It was June of 2016, the end of a bountiful rainy season. The falls had grown to the full width of their boundaries. The avalanching water we had witnessed from below the falls the day prior to our planned visit to Livingstone Island was deafening in its thunder. It was the same majestic Zambezi River where we had seen hippos and alligators, that we were to cross upon the morning.

We would be traveling across the river near the waterfall's edge in boats equipped with two motors, still, though, I dreamed of the precipice. Scratch that, I had nightmares about the precipice. If our boat pilot took us a little too close to the edge for a thrill and the boat's motors failed or were not strong enough against the steady flow of the river above the falls, we would be goners, crushed upon the rocks below. If we capsized upstream, we would be fodder for the crocodiles.

And so too, in the writing of this book there was a wonderful destination, yet there were beastly inhabitants, a chasm of racing water, and an edge where the world ended— where the world might swallow me up. I had not navigated such a river. Did I have a solid boat—and a strong and working engine—did I have a second engine just in case? Did I have the right people with me for the journey? The answer I know now is yes. I had passion, a driving interest in my idea, and my spouse by my side for every step.

I have been driven to help others create a business reflective of themselves that adds value to people's lives and to society. That mission has been my second engine and has propelled me in the face of swift waters and a precipice.

I have seen the edge of the world and continued on. I hope you do too.

Second, listen to what you are learning and adapt as needed as you test your idea and the elements of your business.

It's not enough, it's never enough, to come up with a promising idea and suddenly value is created. Even Einstein, especially Einstein, famous for his thought experiments could not just come up with world-changing ideas that changed the world until his ideas—his hypotheses—were put to the test.

Einstein's theories had to explain real physical phenomena in order to truly gain traction. So too must yours. No entrepreneur has turned an idea into value without taking action, without shaping, evaluating, testing, and proving their idea. SPARK-CLICK-GO lifts the mask of how successful creative entrepreneurs bring their creations to the world.

SPARK-CLICK-GO goes behind the curtain and reveals that Oz is human, just like you. And because you are human, you too can learn how to build and test your ideas, gaining strength along the way, like earning lingots (virtual currency) on Duolingo or gaining new levels in your favorite digital game.

Test your ideas. Even small tests are important across the essential audiences I have highlighted in this book.

It's going to take a big leap for any of us to get into a self-driving car, direct it to an address in a nearby city, and comfortably relax on the freeway—maybe read a book—ensconced in an automobile without a driver. Hell, I wouldn't let my Prius do the parallel parking without my hands surrounding the wheel. I was ready to course correct at any moment.

But maybe if you took me to an empty parking lot in some deserted college campus, like the one my dad took me to when I was learning to drive, where a mistake meant almost nothing and my friend and I could try evasive maneuvers safely, I'd be willing to be driven by a headless driver.

Where is the empty parking lot in your world where you can try out your idea and show what it can do?

If your test "rides" don't work out, adjust. Listen. Get out with potential customers, maybe people on the edge a bit, people open to new solutions and take them to your test track. What happens—what they say and do—can really help you.

I was working on bringing an important new cholesterol medicine to the Canadian market when we came across a boulder in our pathway. My team and I were about to get together with our advisors—specialists in metabolic and endocrine conditions—to share with them the latest information about a drug they were eager to have access to.

One of the reasons our advisors were excited about this medicine was the potential it had to help their sickest patients—the unfortunate people who were dealt a genetic blow that caused extremely high cholesterol levels in their bloodstreams, and lifespans of thirty years on average.

Understandably, then, our advisors were upset when we told them the company had decided to halt development of the highest and most powerful dosage of this new medicine because of safety concerns.

We could have kept this fact from them. We could have just given them the information in a matter-of-fact way, or we could have withheld it until closer to launch, but we chose not to be coy. Instead, we opened up and shared what we had learned with them and sought their advice as to how we might handle this situation from a development and communication point of view.

Our physician advisors were disappointed—reality was falling short of their expectations—but they understood and focused on what the medicine could still offer and how it could benefit their patients, including the sickest among them.

My team and I listened to what our advisors had to say. We listened to understand what they were feeling and what they were saying. Being open allowed for a deeper connection with these important physicians. We left the meeting feeling well equipped for what to do next and feeling much better about the setback. Opening ourselves up created strength for our mission. It created esprit de corps.

That was one step on the way to serving the most patients with that medicine in our market on a per capita basis compared to our peers everywhere else in the world.

So listen and adapt to what opinion leaders and customers are saying about your offering.

Third, launch once your idea has CLICKed with the essential audiences and then improve all aspects of your creative business idea.

- Customers
- Lab people (technical folks)
- Investors (if you have any; if not, you are the investor)
- Creators
- Key opinion leaders

Unless you are a thrill seeker, or you view launching as your real testing ground, do not launch, especially broadly, if your idea has failed to resonate—to CLICK—with at least one person (but preferably many more especially in the case of customers) from your five essential audiences. Launching without this support could come back to haunt you unless you can course correct, as software entrepreneurs can, extremely quickly.

So if there is a gap with an essential audience, especially with your intended customers, go back and fix it, then test again.

If your idea appears to be resonating across your essential five audiences, fantastic, go forward and launch. And make sure to involve people from these essential audiences in your launch. Some of these folks will be allies. They were, after all, among the first to be part of your emerging idea, and they will feel a sense of ownership by being engaged by you.

Once you launch, keep challenging yourself to make your business even more a reflection of yourself, even more valuable to your customers and society, even more driven by your imaginative and original idea(s). Raising the bar is a sure way to sustain your creative business idea. One you can be proud of.

20
Beyond SPARK-CLICK-GO

An early reader asked me, "Doug, what was the main reason you decided to write this book?"

"I wrote *SPARK-CLICK-GO*," I said, "because I wanted to see more people bring their creative business ideas to life." I believe if more people bring more creative business ideas to life, it will be good for society.

I have seen and been a part of many businesses in my life from the early concept phase to full-on success. And I have studied what others who have created successful endeavors, seemingly out of thin air, have done.

Some people are afraid to pursue their ideas. Others have too many ideas and don't know which one to pursue. For some, the perceived lack of something—money, smarts, chutzpah—holds them back.

When I was just out of college at age twenty-three, I borrowed 100 percent of the money I needed for a down payment on a house from my parents and mortgaged the rest. Was it risky? Yah, but I figured I had a steady source of friends who would be looking to rent a room for the next several years (income), and I could fix up the property a bit and pay off the deposit when I sold the house with the profit. It was a calculated risk that worked out well. Plus, we had a ton of fun in that house.

It takes guts to take financial risks just as it can be scary putting an idea out to the world knowing others will judge its value.

My goal with SPARK-CLICK-GO has been to inspire and inform aspiring entrepreneurs like you on how to create value by developing ideas that matter, and to build momentum in your business by reaching guideposts along the path. In so doing, I have sought to reduce or eliminate anxieties you may have and remove obstacles in your way.

Building an offering, and a business model, that you and your team are proud of, that resonates with your customers and opinion leaders, and that delivers on the promises you've made will take risk out of your business, build momentum, and result in investor enthusiasm.

SPARK-CLICK-GO is the creative process applied to business. An idea forms, is shaped and tested in ever more refined ways and with expanding pools of people, and like ripples on a lake, a wave is created. A new urgency exists globally for those waves to fulfill the interests of multiple stakeholders—customers, employees, suppliers, and communities—not just shareholders.

This view comes from the Business Roundtable, an influential group of CEOs from the US—home of winner-take-all capitalism.

As Addisu Lashitew writes for the Brookings Institution, stakeholder capitalism was the theme for the 2020 World Economic Forum in Davos where it was seen as a promising solution to many of the world's (then) current problems.

I come from an industry that is used to satisfying the needs of multiple stakeholders. In *SPARK-CLICK-GO* I have placed an emphasis on creating value for customers *and* to society, so it seems I'm in good company with the world's business leaders.

The soil has never been more fertile to create new businesses. The tools, never better. My hope is to have provided the seeds that will help you bring your creative business idea to life.

Despite, or maybe because of, society's progress, especially in the digital sphere, and ironically within cities, many people feel isolated or unrecognized and have a deep need to connect and to express themselves—hence, when I describe the kind of business I am hoping to see more of in the world, I include the imperative to create a business that is a unique reflection of the person breathing life into it.

SPARK-CLICK-GO is about discovering and focusing on the right problem and developing the right solution.

Anyone can start to shape an idea and share it with others—to take a first step. A first step against the inertia of the status quo. A first step that is neither expensive nor taxing. The key is to take action, almost any action. To check, for example, your understanding of the problem, or find out if your possible solution is desirable among your target customers.

Getting the problem right and being clear about your target audience is essential for several reasons:

- To focus development and testing of your idea
- To benefit your customer
- To make progress for society

Getting the problem right is essential business. Stating the problem clearly during the SPARK phase helps both your customer and your start-up.

In medicine, there is an axiom that the diagnosis is 70 percent of the art—get the diagnosis right and the options for treatment fall into place, and the prognosis becomes clearer.

For start-ups, clarity regarding the problem being solved leads to focused follow-on activities in service of the customer.

But there's another reason getting the problem right is essential business. Progress. Teams that uncover real problems that need to be solved—and then go on to create solutions that resonate with the five essential audiences—move us, all of us, forward. That, in and of itself, is a societal benefit.

Finally, we are all human.

SPARK-CLICK-GO is a method designed to help you reach your goals. Mistakes will be made along the way. Steps will be skipped. Bloopers and blunders will occur.

If you veer, I have set guideposts to bring you back on track.

When you reach the top, send me a note. I'd love to hear your story.

Bonus: How to Find a Creative Business Idea

And you thought you were at the end of the book. What's up with a bonus chapter?

At this point, some of you may be wondering whether you have a winning creative business idea. Others may ask how to come up with one. Ideas reach us in many ways: via our dreams, while singing in the shower, while hanging out with new people, or seeing new parts of the world.

Blake Mycoskie came up with his idea for TOMS shoes—which includes a nonprofit buy-one-give-one model—while traveling in Argentina.

Ideas can come to us in an instant, like a SPARK, and they can percolate in our minds over a weekend, a month, or a lifetime. How an idea reaches us can be a mystery, but it can also be the result of a process actively applied or an experience lived.

When an idea arrives as a flash of insight like a SPARK, jot it down.

As my dad used to say: "Pay attention, there's going to be a test." He had that right.

A flash or a spark of insight about an existing problem or solution that simply appears in the in-box of your mind is manna from heaven. Don't waste it.

Einstein's inspirations may have come quickly, but formulating his thinking took the greater portion of his lifetime. Most of Einstein's work, especially in his early career, was done via thought experiment. He was fascinated with the idea of reasoning his way to a solution. For example, Einstein figured out that a person traveling at the speed of light would not age.

If you could bottle *that* up, you could sell it in galactic portions.

The thing is, even in the Einstein example, where space and time get warped, the fountain-of-youth solution solves a problem that already exists. The problem—or the need—is figuring out how to prevent death and prolong life. It's an ageless desire.

Whether an idea comes to you in a flash—like your next thought—or more slowly, this book is about taking your idea, that SPARK, and shaping it into a form: a product, a solution, a production. Something that others are willing to pay for. Something that is a creative expression of you. It doesn't matter what the business is. What matters is that the idea resonates with you and that someone else finds your offering useful, elegant, or desirable.

If you have an idea already, you shouldn't need this chapter. This chapter is for readers who are seeking a worthwhile idea. This is where you can explore skills and triggers to come up with a new idea and hear the stories of pathfinders whose examples can inspire us.

How do you come up with a worthwhile creative business idea that's right for you?

The two main routes to finding your creative business idea are to

1. Start with the problem or

2. Start with the solution.

For example, if you start with the problem of prolonging human life, easing suffering, or preventing death, how many solutions—how many possible business ideas—can you come up with? How many already exist?

The entire medical field exists to solve this problem. The life insurance business exists because of this problem. Their policies do nothing to increase a person's life, but they give a guy a chance to extend the impact of his life through his offspring should he meet his maker unexpectedly. How about the sunscreen business or the vitamin business? These businesses exist to help people avoid suffering and prolong health.

Vitamins and painkillers, by the way, have become a metaphor in Silicon Valley. Specifically, investors express more interest in businesses where the problem to be solved is acute and pressing, and therefore requires a painkiller, rather than problems less pressing, the ones where a vitamin will do. Cancer is a more pressing problem than male-pattern baldness.

HELP IS ON THE WAY.

An ice-cold beverage at a ball game in the heat of a summer afternoon solves a more pressing problem than tea in the afternoon in the comfort of your air conditioned home.

Keep it simple. Human nature is to move toward pleasure and away from pain.

Begin.

People will often do more to avoid pain than to gain pleasure. Loss aversion, as psychologists call it, is a powerful motivator. It's why parting with cash is painful for most of us—we physically give away something we can see in our wallets and we realize we have less and less of it as the week goes along.

Nothing happens to your credit card when you use it. It doesn't become smaller. Weirdly, it feels like someone else's money at least until the end of the month. And using it more will get you more, won't it? Cash back. Travel. Prestige.

Loss aversion is the driver behind lots of well-known business forms today such as insurance, security systems and services, and healthcare. Most problems that exist today are manifestations of problems humanity has experienced, to varying degrees, since at least the agricultural revolution.

I have identified a wide array of SPARK-CLICK-GO skills that you can use to come up with ideas for possible businesses. Whether taking a problem-driven or a solution-driven approach, you can tap into these skills to help get you to the germ—to the SPARK—of an idea. Some skills can be used either when starting from the problem and working toward your creative business idea, or when starting with an existing solution to get to your creative business idea.

If you use any of these skills to find a creative business idea, I assure you they will mesh with your interest—and possibly talents and background—and with something you would want to bring into the world. How do I know? Because you will be there when you think of these ideas.

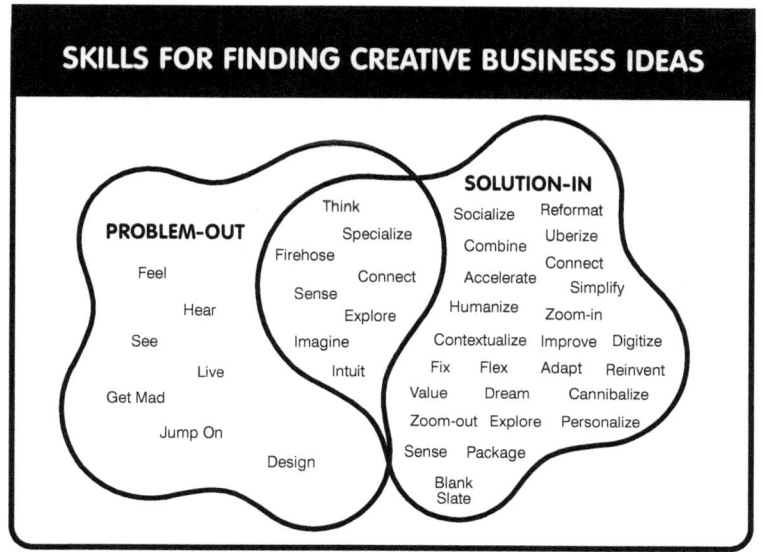

IDENTIFY A PROBLEM OR BUILD ON/ CHANGE/ IMPROVE AN EXISTING SOLUTION TO COME UP WITH PROMISING IDEAS

Steve Jobs said, "Your time is limited, so don't waste it living someone else's life."

I would love to write a chapter about each of these skills. I started doing that but realized that might not be the most valuable use of your time, so, instead, I've written briefly about most of them in this chapter.

As a reminder, this chapter is really valuable if you have not already found a potential idea to develop.

Here are the skills with a bit of color added so you can picture my meaning:

FEEL. Empathize with someone—feel their pain—see their need and come up with something that can reduce or eliminate that pain.

Anne Budra did just that when she became aware of a problem in her electoral area. The problem: University students who were away from their home provinces (Canada) were unable to vote in an important federal election in the province in which they were going to school because it was outside of their voting jurisdiction.

Listening to their concerns, Anne wondered how she would feel not being able to participate in an important federal election. And she thought about her own grandchildren and about the importance of enfranchising all voters, including young people.

The solution Anne came up with—bring the ballot to the people. This solution brought special ballots directly to campus, something that had never been done before. Anne worked with her special ballot team to bring access to the ballots containing the names of all the candidates in a student's home jurisdiction directly to campus and worked out the procedures to verify and have these ballots sent to the appropriate collection offices. The student votes were counted, and this became a model throughout Canada. SPARK-CLICK-GO!

Temie Giwa-Tuboson created a business in Nigeria called LifeBank to rush much needed blood from donor banks by motorcycle to maternity wards, thereby avoiding traffic gridlock and saving lives in the process.

As Giwa-Tuboson told Saleem Reshamwala on his podcast *PinDrop*, she started the business because she saw a young woman needlessly lose a baby in childbirth. By talking to the docs and nurses, she figured out that hemorrhaging was a major cause of fetal death to women in childbirth in hospitals in Lagos.

LifeBank has expanded from the transferring of blood in Lagos, the initial SPARK of the business idea in 2016, to supplying blood, blood products, oxygen, and vaccines across Africa. The business's goal is to save one million lives.

LifeBank started because of Giwa-Tuboson's compassion for women in Nigeria, a country not her own.

DIGITIZE. Take something from the physical or human world and put it online. Lots of spaces remain open to digitizing. True, the shopping mall, or at least the products found there, have been put online. And yes, libraries are online as are photo albums, matchmakers—almost everything it seems, including connected objects. But a ton of ideas remain. Zoom has brought the meeting room to the cloud and simultaneously ended the need to put the chairs back in place and vacuum the cookie crumbs in the conference room at day's end. What can you digitize?

THINK. Think about opportunities for creative business ideas and the solutions. Jack Dorsey thought up Twitter. He thought it might be cool for people to keep their friends up to date with their goings-on by posting status updates via SMS. Later his cofounders, including Noah Glass, became fascinated with the social grouping concept around which the idea was shaped. Do you have a concept that could become a business? Maybe a home genetic profiling service or a drive-thru flower store?

EXPLORE. Take apart an existing industry and look for gaps to fill. Get together with customers and see how they use existing offerings. Pick a field and dive in. Read about it. Research it. Interview key players.

HUMANIZE. This is a counterpoint to Digitize. SP Books produces limited edition, large format book manuscripts that seek to preserve the look and feel provided by a physical draft. As cofounder Jessica Nelson told the BBC, "We feel strongly about the importance for today's reader to be able to connect with the author's hand and delve directly into the manuscript."

Is there a product or service that so many people receive online now that they are desperate for the human touch? Instead of a dating app, create something more meaningful for singles, like retreats.

Ask yourself, what is the emotion driving the human need that your offering could better satisfy? For example, people take time to prepare meals for one another to show their love. Think of a parent and their children. Therefore, creating an automaton to cook at home as a substitute for a parent's love will not satisfy a key part of the child's need, the need for love, even though the automaton provides the physical sustenance of a meal. And to the parent, an offering like this might not be desirable either since the work of cooking, in this context, is not work at all, but rather an act of love.

IMPROVE. How can you improve on an existing product or business, or how could you improve or enhance someone's life? Each of these prompts can lead you to new creative business ideas. Start with a solution you are familiar with or a group of people you know well professionally or personally.

DESIGN. Start with the context of a problem, a goal, and some constraints to come up with two or three options for a solution. Constraints might include a durability goal, number of moving parts, or ease of use.

SIMPLIFY. Speaks to how products or services that do one thing, but do that one thing really well, can flourish in the market. Cinnabon Bakery is an example. Oil-change places for car service is another.

COMBINE. Are there two or more technologies, products, or services out there you could combine to create a new offering. How about a nail salon/blow-dry bar? What about a drone with a camera? You get the idea. How about a car wash/barber shop?

HEAR. Listening, really listening, to customers and employees from fields you are currently involved with or interested in can yield a lot of valuable ideas. Cherry Garcia, the finest flavor of ice cream ever created by Ben & Jerry's Ice Cream was suggested to them directly by a fan, Jane Williamson, in 1986. She sent Ben and Jerry a postcard that said:

> Dear Ben & Jerry's:
>
> We're great fans of the Grateful Dead and we're great fans of your ice cream. Why don't you make a cherry flavor and call it Cherry Garcia? You know it will sell because Dead paraphernalia always sells. We are talking good business sense here, plus it will be a real hoot for the fans.

Ben & Jerry's liked the idea, so they developed the flavor. Cherry Garcia got a thumbs-up from Jerry Garcia and became the company's top seller for a decade—I'm sure they're eternally grateful.

It pays to listen sometimes—to listen and then to act.

SEE. Quite simply, see a problem in need of a better solution. Can you create a better solution using today's technologies, know-how, and knowledge? Or paint a picture for a business, like a computer on every desk. That vision can prompt you and others to develop a compelling, long-lasting business idea.

JUMP ON. This is for the opportunist. The Falcon Golf X1 Pin Ball (hands-free) Retriever, which allowed golfers to collect their balls without touching the flagpole, and courses to offer safer playing environments during the COVID-19 pandemic, is an example of jumping on an opportunity. When you were a kid and it snowed like hell, did you grab a snow shovel and go around to neighbors selling your snow-removal services? Why not?

"Danger gathers upon our path. We cannot afford—we have no right—to look back—we must look forward," said Winston Churchill in 1936 who is sometimes credited with saying, "A good crisis should never be wasted."

Crises hold the opportunity for changes in people's expectations and behaviors just as we've seen, for example, with more people and businesses shifting to remote work during the COVID-19 crisis. Or businesses shifting to manufacture hand sanitizer and face masks.

The benefit goes to those who move swiftly forward.

CANNIBALIZE. For existing business owners. Do you have an existing offering that you could improve on and replace your existing offerings with? Do it now or someone else will.

SOCIALIZE. Is there a problem you know about that might be well solved by the crowd? Put it out there. Is there a business now that could be enhanced by adding a social component? The yellow pages were once the go-to tool for finding business phone numbers and locations. The ads caught the attention of potential customers, but what they lacked was any information from customers' experiences. Enter Yelp. Shopify is another example with a first-rate platform upon which to create your online store enhanced by user-generated content in the form of reviews.

UBERIZE. What is the Uber for X problem? In its essence, Uber is a specific service delivered on demand almost anywhere (and now Uber delivers takeout food). Can you do that with a different service? You don't have to use Uber as your analog. Take almost any successful idea out there and see if you can apply it to a new area. For example, Curves created a comfortable place where women could work out. Can you Curv-ize an idea for women? How about auto repair shops? Already done, but not to scale.

FIREHOSE. The idea here is to take an output from one business and make something new from it like making building materials from old tires, or making disposable kitchenware out of sugarcane pulp, one of the food industry's largest waste products, as Hongli (Julie) Zhu of Northeastern University and her colleagues are doing according to Good News Network.

CONNECT. Think buyers and sellers, performers and audience, freelancers and producers, supply and demand and how your business can help both sides of the equation by creating a platform, an exchange, essentially a marketplace.

Spotify is a sound example. The record industry that held all the licensing rights to songs was collapsing because of illegal digital downloading. Piracy was immensely popular. Spotify offered a way to match suppliers of songs to the listeners by creating an easy-to-use alternative to piracy.

When I was in college, a friend of mine, Steve Upton, and I created a service where sellers and buyers of used textbooks could find each other and make a sale.

LIVE. From your personal or professional life, you see a pattern, a problem, a need for a solution *and* you decide you are the one to solve that problem. When you live with the people experiencing a problem, you have inhabited the tribe. The best way to do that is by being a member of the tribe or group. Next best is embedding yourself in a tribe that is not your own. Far beyond that is reading about a group of people or the responses of people to a survey from that group.

Tom Oswald was on duty as an NYPD firefighter when he and his company were called to a five-alarm fire in the Bronx on a windy but otherwise normal day in 1994.

Earlier, a man had fallen asleep while smoking a cigarette on his bed, the window to his north-facing living room left open.

As he awakened to smoke and fire, the man attempted to put the fire out, but the flames leaped from his mattress to his furniture and bedroom walls. The flames were now raging beyond the man's control, so in fear and desperation he rushed into the hallway and for the exits. In his haste he left the door to his apartment open.

A draft rushed through the man's apartment created by the gaping apartment door and the open window. Firefighters call this a wind-driven fire. The fire is now an inferno.

A neighbor on the same floor, a woman, heard the alarm and quickly grabbed her purse, her wedding album, and a few personal items before exiting her apartment. The heated gases and smoke arrested her on the threshold even though the flames were the length of a football field away. She did not make it past her doorway.

Later, as Tom and his teammates were debriefing about the fire, Tom said: "If we could have blocked the window on the north side of the smoking man's apartment with something—maybe even a piece of plywood—we could have sucked the oxygen from that blaze, brought it under control, and maybe saved that woman's life."

As Tom told me years later, at his workplace on Long Island, many firefighters agreed. Members of his unit spoke about this fire for weeks after it was snuffed out. The tragedy weighed on them all. Lots of people saw or heard about the dead woman and agreed something could be done better next time, but no one acted. So Tom did.

Tom took it upon himself to fight future wind-driven apartment fires by inventing the KO Fire Curtain—a flexible device firefighters place over open or smashed windows while a fire is in progress.

The device stops drafts, withstands the wear and tear of being tossed down stairs, is heat and fire resistant, and is portable—the result of many design iterations some of which were informed by Tom's experience as a windsurfer.

Tom and a partner created the KO Fire Curtain device and a business to produce and sell it out of the ashes of tragedy—something they lived with on the job all too often.

PACKAGE. This is an age-old approach. We humans love convenience and we love affiliation. My wife and I buy sparkling water bottled in Bergamo, Italy. Why? What's wrong with Maine or Vermont, Quebec or Claremont? Maybe it's because we love northern Italy. Maybe it's the taste or the association with cafe dinners with a red and white checkered tablecloth in the streets of Modena.

The point is almost anything can be packaged and sold with or without extensive branding. Another beautiful Italian example: Acqua Dell' Elba. Purchase this perfume while on the isle of Elba in Tuscany (the beautiful island Napoleon retreated to before marching on Paris) and you take away some of the fresh air and scents of flowers from its mountain meadows.

ACCELERATE. Is there a proven business or business process that you can make faster? Why not do it? In Silicon Valley, they look for a tenfold or 10X improvement on at least one key factor. Why? Because that will provide enough leverage to overcome the power of inertia.

SENSE. Did you know your smartphone has a barometer? An accelerometer? The world is becoming full of sensors. How can you use one to create a business?

INTUIT. Why not follow your intuition to come up with an idea? Start with something that feels right to you as a creative business idea, then start to shape and test it out.

CONTEXTUALIZE. Look at the whole experience offered by an existing product or service. Identify what the user does, or is forced to do, before, during, and after consumption to come up with ways to deliver the same goods or service but in innovative ways that add value or eliminate costs and hassles for the user.

Could you create a business that provides solutions before or after what that customer does now? Is there an opportunity after the fact? For example, third-party warranties pitch themselves as security post-purchase. That is a profitable business (though almost never worth the fees for purchasers).

REFORMAT. Take an existing solution and put it into a different form. For example, take a book and make a movie of it or a musical as Lin-Manuel Miranda did with Ron Chernow's book *Alexander Hamilton*. To be clear, LMM brought a ton of creativity and himself to the idea of creating a musical from the bones of the story, deciding key elements to tell, and which to leave out. It was not a simple transposing—quite the opposite.

Video is a leading format (form-factor) today. What could you re-create as video from a different format? Another prompt: What can you take that is today delivered physically and deliver it via telepresence? Teladoc, a leading provider of telemedicine services, provides online visits with physicians and is a stand-out example of reformatting. Let your creativity run wild with this method of coming up with ideas for businesses.

GET MAD. This is one of my favorites. It's the emotion of annoyance or anger as the SPARK. You see something being done so poorly you just know you can do it better. Maybe terrible taxi ride experiences were the motivation for ride-sharing companies? Is there something that ticks you off that you can improve on? How about airlines? Neil Young was so ticked off at the quality of digital music he created his own brand called PonoPlayer, which began as a stand-alone music player and online store and morphed into a streaming service and audio archive service XStream.

If you find yourself saying: "There has got to be a better way," maybe this will lead you to an idea you will have passion for.

FIX. How many times have you seen a gap in a product or service and your armchair critic comes alive but then nothing happens? Come on. Take it to the next level. Sketch out a solution.

FLEX. Did you know that the drug minoxidil that we now know as Rogaine was originally developed to treat high blood pressure? It was. So too was a little blue pill with one side effect that stood out in male subjects—erections—while it was being studied as a blood pressure–lowering agent in the lungs. Hello, Viagra.

The enterprise collaborations app Slack was created because the online multiplayer game that Stewart Butterfield and cofounders were working on as Tiny Speck did not pan out, yet the expanding team found that the internal communication tool they created did work, and others who tried it seemed to like it too. As of mid-2020, Slack was valued at more than $15 billion.

ADAPT. Can you take a product or service that has an application in one area and modify it so that it solves a problem in another? Maybe something that is aimed at commercial contractors can be made into a DIY solution, for example? Or something used for business could be made for consumers.

"NOBODY'S BUYING OUR GAMES BUT MAN THAT SYSTEM WE BUILT TO GET STUFF DONE SURE IS COOL."

A famous example is taking GPS, which was designed for the military and re-creating it as a consumer product. Someone had to ask the "what if?" question.

When I was an advisor to a tech accelerator out of Livermore, California, there was a young military guy fresh back from duty overseas whose idea was to adapt technology used for military surveillance—presumably of enemy combatant locations—to the monitoring of crops via small plane surveillance and advanced computing. The company, TerrAvion, attracted funding, created a working prototype, and successfully sold subscriptions to farmers. Maybe this is a whole new class of business. Surveillance as a Service? Scary.

Or why not take a product from another country as Blake Mycoskie did when he brought alpargatas shoes from his travels in Argentina and started TOMS, and what many countries do to localize movies by dubbing them to another language or adding subtitles so viewers in more places in the world can enjoy shows like *Fauda,* an Israeli series shot in Hebrew or *Trapped* filmed in Iceland.

Adapting from nature is what the Wright brothers did with wing designs inspired from birds, which led to manned flight, then commercial airlines.

Nature-inspired design is called biomimicry, and in the translational medicine world, researchers like Jeffrey Karp and his team at The Karp Lab in Cambridge, Massachusetts, are using it to create innovations like spider web–inspired medical tape and porcupine-inspired needles.

PERSONALIZE. Make a solution your own. Brand it. Deliver it in a way that is unique to you.

ZOOM-IN. Can you take something that is offered generally and specialize with it for a particular audience? Cases for smartphones were and are a big business. When they first came out, they were functional, and the focus was on having cases that worked with each phone. They may have been offered for men and women. Eventually, the offerings became more tailored to specific groups like teens and sports fans. Can you do it in a different realm?

ZOOM-OUT. Take something peculiar to one group now and generalize it.

VALUE. Here is where you dissect an industry and figure out the value chain. Once you have the anatomy figured out, work backward to see if there's a place to disrupt the chain. Redfin in real estate is an example of this. They offered similar information to what standard real estate agents deliver at lower commission rates. Redfin realized there was a lot of money being made by agents on commissions despite an MLS system, which provides immense transparency on listings, sales, average number of days on market, and more. Upstart online book seller Bookshop is trying to blunt Amazon's market power by directing higher affiliate revenues to independent bookstores.

Maybe you can do something like going direct with an offering in a space where everyone is using a distributor and therefore giving profit away. What opportunities can you uncover?

DREAM. You've been dreaming all your life. What is your subconscious trying to tell you? Maybe you've woken up in the pitch black quiet of the night still dreaming and thought to yourself something crazy like: "Wow, this Time Machine I just figured out how to build is mind blowing."

Do you have a way for keeping dreams like that alive? Why not? What about dreams you may have held in your mind for a long time like creating your own business for people combining your love of traveling and teaching? Either of these types of dreams can lead you to a creative business idea.

REINVENT. Imagine something that you loved during your childhood but is now fading. Can you bring it back to life in a modern way? Cirque du Soleil is an example of this—strip out the animals, increase the acrobatic acts and the sophistication of the big top performance through costumes, create a theme, a musical score, choreography, and story, and BINGO you have reinvented a gem from your childhood. Make it an attractive series of dazzling shows and people will enjoy it as a modern night out full of breathtaking entertainment.

What can you reinvent for today's audience? Arcades possibly? Mini golf?

IMAGINE. This is about imagining a solution as if no others existed at the moment given all the tools available. It's about starting without the old methods of doing things. For example, creating a car company not based on fossil fuels or not geared toward personal ownership.

BLANK SLATE. How could you offer something people already buy or meet a need people have that is being fulfilled by a business today without its constraints? Isn't this how Airbnb came up with a platform for people with extra space to match up to folks looking for a space to stay in the short term? They removed the need to build and manage all those properties.

ACTIVE VERB. This is your chance to come up with your own skill. What works for you? Did I miss a key skill? Research. Read. Dig, as in dig into a problem until you expose its root.

And who doesn't need a SPARK? The first date my wife and I had has been a spark that has fueled thirty years of marriage and counting. It was a three-hour lunch at a quaint Italian restaurant in Calgary, Alberta, where we first hit it off. While a marriage is a special kind of a partnership and is not a business, it contains some similarities like vision, compatibility, shared commitment, and more. At that lunch we started to share what we wanted in life and possible directions.

Now go out and put some of these skills to use. If reading is your thing, read about an area of interest. Ask Mr. Google if he knows the top ten problems affecting people in a given field of interest. Put yourself in the shoes of a customer—do a ride along with a customer or job shadow someone working in the area. You get the picture. Pick a method each day or week and try it on.

And take a notebook—your phone—with you.

At the end of your sleuthing, look back and reflect on your observations. Are there one or two problems that intrigue you? Is there a solution out there you think you can improve upon? Is there a technological solution that could be deployed against a need by you?

Pick these and take a moment to flesh out what they could look like as a creative business idea. Bounce them around in your brain a bit.

You've now read about a number of skills that could lead you to a creative business idea. I encourage you to use as many or as few of these as you find appealing. Generate as many ideas as you can. You'll have time to assess them later.

Now start back at the beginning of this book where you can read about how to gauge whether your idea is a good one and how to shape it into something more than just an idea. Find out how to move it along the SPARK-CLICK-GO Journey on its way to becoming an exemplary business that is a reflection of who you are.

Reflect & Act

- There are two main ways of coming up with ideas for a creative business: Start with the *problem* or start with the existing *solution*.

- Within the broad categories of problem-driven or solution-driven, SPARK-CLICK-GO identifies the specific skills you can use to come up with ideas. Pick a skill, or several skills, to work with over the coming days. Write down any ideas that come up. Try as many of the skills as possible until you come up with a promising idea.

- Silicon Valley's categorization of solutions as either painkillers or vitamins offers other starting points to get you thinking and acting. Use them to come up with a promising idea if you prefer.

SPARK-CLICK-GO FAQs

Q1. What is the SPARK-CLICK-GO Journey?

A1. SPARK-CLICK-GO is a process to help aspiring entrepreneurs bring their creative business ideas to life.

Q2. What is a creative business idea and how does it differ from a regular business idea?

A2. A creative business idea (CBI) deploys imaginative, or original ideas, to deliver value for others and for society profitably, while uniquely reflecting and benefiting its creators. Use of imaginative or original ideas pushes you to create a business that will stand out while delivering value for others *and* society. A true creative business idea benefits society in a meaningful way in addition to benefiting customers, creators, and investors. That means you need to design and run the business in a manner that is sensitive to the environment and attentive to the quality of life of people—and other living beings—in its orbit.

Creating a business that uniquely reflects and benefits its creators means you are building aspects of your personality and passions into the equation. This should result in a more fulfilling business and one that you will be more likely to stick with in good times and in bad.

Q3. Does SPARK-CLICK-GO apply to all types of businesses?

A3. The SPARK-CLICK-GO Journey applies to any creative business idea. It was derived from looking across a wide variety of businesses and pulling out common elements. It applies to technical and nontechnical business areas and to regulated and nonregulated sectors alike. One way to improve your approach to developing a strong creative business idea is to borrow approaches from other fields and apply them to your idea. I encourage you to experiment.

Q4. Would I need to follow all of the steps in SPARK-CLICK-GO to successfully launch a new business?

A4. No, you could go right from SPARK to GO, and many people do. In this case you are not really skipping the CLICK testing and development phase altogether, you are just testing your prototype in the great big world. Your laboratory or test kitchen is just a little bit bigger. If you fail—you fail big, and fast.

Q5. Does SPARK-CLICK-GO only apply to new businesses?

A5. No! You could use it to take your business in a new direction, or to make it more a reflection of you, or to build in a societal benefit, to add a new business line, or to improve your business model.

Q6. I have a lot of commitments; how do I start a new business?

A6. Everyone's situation is different so no single answer will satisfy everyone on this question. That said, one of the tenets of the SPARK-CLICK-GO Journey is that small steps can really help build momentum and reduce the risks around the viability of your creative business idea. Small steps need not cost a lot of money, nor take all of your time.

One way to start a business is to adopt the artist's model, as Jordan Rich (host of the *On MIC* podcast and partner in Chart Productions) put it to me, meaning your commissioned work—your regular day job—is your main gig, but you always have your own projects in the corner so you can work on them "between the raindrops." I love that image. Thank you, Jordan.

Acknowledgments

A creative endeavor, as with a creative business idea, may be the initial concept of one person, but it takes a lot of people to bring it into reality.

Many people have shaped me along the way, and many have worked directly or indirectly on this book, for which I am grateful beyond words.

Philippe Latapie is one of the first innovators I discussed my idea for this book with, including the title. I count Phil as a friend and colleague. He is always ready to talk about innovation or to make introductions and to brainstorm. Phil was an early manuscript reader as well, adding insightful comments and examples to explore.

Thankful too am I, and Yoda, to Adam Lorant. Adam is a dear classmate from my Western University days. He has had a dynamic and successful career as an entrepreneur and investor in Vancouver, Canada. Adam read an early manuscript and more than any other person provided expert commentary that has made this book better. Thank you, Adam.

Dr. Danny Lange, serial MedTech entrepreneur and professor, Technion Institute of Technology, Israel, graciously offered to read several chapters and provided many helpful observations. Thank you, Danny.

I want to thank Jane Friedman, publishing wizard, who listened to my aspirations for the book, and who provided me with the idea to pursue an editor early on for what is called in the trade, developmental editing. That led me to my editor Sandra Wendel who has been my guiding light on this project. Sandy took me in, like a lost puppy in the rain, dried me off, gave me sustenance, and got me set on the right path.

Thank you to Matt Davis for setting the visual look for the book and for the striking book cover, illustrations, and diagrams. Megan McCullough of Chicago has been my interior design wizard. Thank you, Megan.

I owe a debt of gratitude to Debby Peoples, who hosts the Cold Spring Harbor writers' group, as well as to Mimy Mazzarella and the wonderful writers in that group whose fellowship and encouragement made a real and lasting impact on me as a writer. Keep writing and creating.

Because this book is a reflection of whom I am, to truly thank people involved for its creation, I have to thank all those who have shaped me professionally and personally. So, thank you to the people I have worked with in early-stage companies, on commercial corporate teams, and in my consulting role (and that means StratX).

I thank James Murphy as well, fellow author, whose Crime Mystery Webinar Series from Northern Ireland kept me intrigued and inspired and brought fresh perspectives to my storytelling. Thank you to the writers in the group too for sharing your work.

William Zinsser, speaking to me, as if one-on-one through his book, *On Writing Well*, taught me a lot and encouraged me to bring myself to the page, since that is all a writer really has.

To Jordan Rich, fellow author and friend, I'm happy to be sharing the book writing journey with you.

Thank you to all the people who helped me set up interviews: Bill Russell, Alan Slavik, Juan Carlos Garcia

Estrada. And to all the people I did interview: Tom Oswald, Jordan Rich, Hayde López Rodríguez, Skip Klintworth, and Adam Lorant. And thank you to all the people whose stories I have told here who are out there making things happen, dedicating a part of themselves to creating businesses others can benefit from.

On the personal side, my thanks to my mom and dad, Midge and Murray Ross, and to my brothers and sisters in blood, and in law.

I've been doubly lucky in the parenting category. My parents encouraged me in every endeavor throughout my life, including when I wanted to become a doctor, through wanting to quit college, to my turn toward business and a start in sales. I say I've been doubly lucky because my in-laws, Anne and Al Budra, too, have been incredibly supportive, even though my unsolicited proposal for their daughter's hand in marriage came a bit more quickly than they may have been ready for.

I am blessed to have friends and family whom I cherish and are a source of strength in Canada, the U.S., the U.K., and beyond. Thank you for your support and fellowship.

Going way back, thinking of my teachers, I have to say, Mr. Hobson, Central Memorial High School English teacher, was an inspiration, as was my seventh-grade drama teacher. Thank you for stoking my creative side.

I want to thank my sons, Alex, Nick, and Ben, for their humor, curiosity, outlook on life and for their valuable comments on the manuscript. I'm proud of the people they are and very proud to be their father.

To the people who helped me choose the book cover art and commented on the book title, thank you.

Finally, the book would literally not have been possible without my wife Bridget's constant support and encouragement. One of her ex-bosses said of Bridget, that of all the people he might want beside him in a fox hole, it would be her. I could not say it better. As my first and finest reader she was always ready with a positive suggestion. She saw the vision for this book and has been the catalyst that has brought it to life. She is the reason I have been able to pursue my dreams. Thank you, honey.

About the Author

Douglas Ross is a writer, strategy and innovation advisor, entrepreneur, and mentor to early-stage entrepreneurs. He is currently part of the leadership team of a start-up seeking to disrupt the diagnostic market and has been among the cofounders at two software start-ups. Doug has led, or been part of, numerous teams delivering innovation and visioneering workshops with top-tier clients.

In his corporate career he was responsible for pipeline products, commercialization, launch, and marketed products from niche to blockbuster. Doug is into setting difficult goals and going after them.

He was a misfit at MBA school. Instead of thinking about Black Scholes mathematical models and risk adjusted cost of capital, he was interested in marketing, consumer behavior, and innovation—natural extensions of his psychology undergraduate degree.

Doug grew up on classic rock and modern folk music and is a student of the creative process. He enjoys sharing inspiring stories about how business, technical, musical, and other creations came into being. He spent his early years in Canada making peanut butter cups, mowing lawns, and shoveling snow—anything to make a buck.

Doug is married and lives in Boston, a city impossibly innovative and good at sports. He is most proud of his three adult sons, Alex, Nick, and Ben—creations his wife, Bridget, made possible, as with most things in his life.

Contact Doug at www.sparkclickgo.com.